LANGUAGE AND LITERACY SERIES

Dorothy S. Strickland, Celia Genishi, and Donna Alvermann SERIES EDITORS

ADVISORY BOARD: RICHARD ALLINGTON, KATHRYN AU,
BERNICE CULLINAN, COLETTE DAIUTE, ANNE HAAS DYSON, CAROLE EDELSKY,
JANET EMIG, SHIRLEY BRICE HEATH, CONNIE JUEL, SUSAN LYTLE, TIMOTHY SHANAHAN

* Volumes with an asterisk following the title are a part of the NCRLL set: Approaches to Language and Literacy Research, edited by JoBeth Allen and Donna Alvermann.

READING THE MEDIA

Media Literacy in High School English

Renee Hobbs

Teachers College, Columbia University
New York and London

INTERNATIONAL
Reading Association
800 BARKSDALE ROAD, PO BOX 8139
NEWARK, DE 19714-8139, USA (302) 731-1600
www.reading.org

Published simultaneously by Teachers College Press, 1234 Amsterdam Avenue, New York, NY 10027 and The International Reading Association, 800 Barksdale Road, Newark, DE 19714.

Library of Congress Cataloging-in-Publication Data

Reading the media: media literacy in high school English / Renee Hobbs.
  p. cm. — (Language and literacy series)
Includes bibliographical references and index.
ISBN-13: 097-8807747391 (hardcover : alk. paper)
ISBN-10: 0-8077-4739-4 (hardcover : alk. paper)
ISBN-13: 097-8807747384 (pbk. : alk. paper)
ISBN-10: 0-8077-4738-6 (pbk. : alk. paper)
  1. Mass media in education—United States. 2. Media literacy—United States. 3. Critical thinking. 4. Media literacy—Study and teaching (Secondary). 5. Mass media—Study and teaching. I. Title.
  LB1043.H628 2007
  302.23071'2—dc22

2006022620

ISBN-13: 978-0-8077-4738-4 (paper) ISBN-10: 0-8077-4738-6 (paper)
ISBN-13: 978-0-8077-4739-1 (cloth) ISBN-10: 0-8077-4739-4 (cloth)

IRA inventory number 9217

Printed on acid-free paper
Manufactured in the United States of America

14 13 12 11   8 7 6 5 4 3 2

Contents

Acknowledgments

My whole life, I have been fascinated by the kind of work that teachers do when they use media and technology in the classroom. When English faculty at Concord High School in New Hampshire described their new initiative in media literacy and invited me to develop a research project on their work, I leaped at the opportunity. I first learned about this program in the summer of 1998 when some of the teachers attended an urban education staff development seminar that I offered at Clark University in Worcester, Massachusetts, entitled Teaching the Humanities in a Media Age. By then, their curriculum plan had already been approved by the school board, and the teachers were spending the summer developing curriculum materials, purchasing instructional resource materials, and developing their own knowledge and skills. The teachers at Concord High School invited me to come and observe their classrooms, interview them, and develop a research project to assess the value of the new curriculum on student learning. It seemed like a perfect opportunity to develop what is now called *design-based research*, a long-term enterprise involving intentional design coupled to empirical research and theorizing about what takes place in authentic contexts. Such work incorporates mixed-methods research in order to cross traditional boundary lines both methodologically and theoretically (Bell, 2004). The research I present in this book is, to my knowledge, the first large-scale qualitative and empirical measurement of the implementation of media literacy at the district level in the United States.

Many teachers have shaped my thinking about media literacy over the years. Professor Barbra Morris at the University of Michigan ignited my interest in media literacy as an undergraduate; Gavriel Salomon and David Perkins at Harvard helped me reflect on the role of symbol systems in the learning process; Barbara Flagg let me teach graduate courses on multimedia evaluation that led me to develop the Harvard Institute on Media Education, where I first got a chance to meet more than 200 talented practitioners, advocates, and scholars from all across the United States. Thanks go to Faith Rogow, Donna Alvermann, Catherine Gourley, Cyndy Scheibe, David Considine, Frank Baker, Elana Rosen, LaTanya Bailey Jones, Tessa Jolls, Kathleen Tyner, Bob Kubey, Karon Sherarts, Brian Primack, William Kist, Bill Costanzo, Sut Jhally, David Bruce, Elizabeth Thoman, Steve Goodman, Bill Tally, James

Potter, Mary Christel, Ellen Krueger, Art Silverblatt, and my colleagues at the Alliance for a Media Literate America (AMLA). My international colleagues—Chris Worsnop, Barry Duncan, Pier Cesare Rivoltella, Damiano Felini, Alberto Pellai, John Pungente, David Buckingham, Cary Bazalgette, Roxana Morduchowitz, Silvia Bacher, Thierry DeSmedt, Robyn Quin, and the late Andrew Hart—have stimulated my ideas on media education over many years.

The teachers and school administrators in Billerica, Massachusetts, were among the first to nurture my curiosity about the possibilities of creating a learning community where teachers and students across the K–12 curriculum could explore the ways that media texts, tools, and technologies shape our sense of personal and social identity in a complex mediated cultural environment. John Katsoulis generously invited me to join the Billerica educational community and offered me 3 years to work with many talented teachers including Bill Walsh, Jeanne Brusseau, Alex Camilio, Roger Goldsmith, and Jack Locke. Damian Curtiss, then the K–12 Language Arts Department head at Billerica, was the first person who helped me recognize that media literacy was an expanded conceptualization of literacy, and his perspectives on the relationship between literacy, technology, media studies, and school reform were enlightening. At Dennis-Yarmouth High School on Cape Cod, I was grateful for the opportunity to spend many summers teaching media literacy, learning along with the creative and talented faculty of that school district. Bruce MacPherson and Julia Johnson supported my research on approaches to integrating media literacy at the district level.

In working with media professionals at the Discovery Channel, I was able to support the growth of media literacy by spreading the word to larger and larger numbers of teachers and students. Judith McHale, Nancy Brien, Linda Brown, Carrie Passmore, and Don Baer were instrumental to this work at the Discovery Channel. Nancy Grasmick at the Maryland State Department of Education and Muffet Livaudais at the Texas Education Agency showed me the strategic value of integrating media literacy into the K–12 curriculum as a means to reach all learners with the highest expectations.

At Clark University, Professor Sarah Michaels generously encouraged me to develop a summer institute for urban educators, where I first met the teachers who would lead me to Concord High School. Over the years, Bob Cowan, Joanne McGlynn, Elizabeth York, Christine Oskar-Poisson, Valerie Aubry, and Mike Robb Grieco were helpful in sharing the complexity of what was happening at Concord High School. They welcomed me into their classrooms and shared their own passion, questions, and creativity. I acknowledge Concord Superintendent of Schools Christine Rath and all the Concord English teachers who have taught English 11 over the past 9 years, including Heather Ouellette-Cygan, Michael Robinson, Linda Lawson, Tara Connolly, Denise Pariseau, Denise Fournier, Robert Pingree, Diane Salisbury, Kristin Smith, Kaileen Gleason, James Doneski, and Tim Doughtery.

I'm particularly grateful to Richard Frost, Jasmin Sung, Dorothy Frey, and Lesley Johnson, who assisted with many aspects of the data gathering process. At Temple University, Jeff Rush, Dave Marshall, and Sherri Hope Culver inspired my love of Philadelphia. Dean Concetta Stewart has supported a vision of the School of Communications and Theater as a place that emphasizes the value of cross-disciplinary scholarship in media studies.

My husband, Randy, has been a vibrant source of encouragement, and my children, Roger and Rachel, now growing up as media-literate teens, are a continual inspiration to me. I dedicate this book to my parents, John and Rosemarie Shilcusky, who through their own lives have shown me the importance of integrity, laughter, and love.

PART I

MEDIA LITERACY IN CONTEXT

Chapter 1

Reading the Media in High School

It's nearly lunchtime at Concord High School in the fall of 1999, and students are talking about television. But it's not the usual patter of opinions about celebrity fashion, football scores, or who saw the latest episode of *The Real World*, the kind of talk that happens at the edges of class periods, in the hallways, in the gym, or in the lunchroom. The conversation is happening inside the classroom in English 11, a required course taken by all 11th-grade students at the high school. As part of a lesson on the construction of realism in film and television, students have been given a note card with the name of a television program on it. On the white board at the front of the room, the teacher has drawn a long horizontal line, and written the words *realistic* on the left end of the line and *unrealistic* on the right end. As students go to the front of the room and mark the name of their show on the continuum, they explain what specific aspects of the show seem realistic or unrealistic, and they provide an explanation and rationale for their opinions.

Cherelle, a brown-haired teen, stands at the front of the classroom and writes *Roseanne* just to the left of the name *Growing Pains* that has been previously placed on the continuum by another student. She explains her decision:

> *Roseanne* is unrealistic because it's a comedy, and they have to exaggerate to make it funny. But I put it as more realistic than *Growing Pains*, because part of the reason it is funny is because Roseanne says a lot of things that people actually think sometimes. She says things that real people really feel but don't actually say out loud. And also, the characters aren't all beautiful and perfect, either, so that's why I consider this show somewhat realistic.

Next up is Danielle, who goes up to put *Saved by the Bell* on the chart. But she's not nearly so confident in her explanation, saying only, "I think that most of the stuff they have in this show is real. It happened. But the way it's presented is too perfect."

The teacher asks, "What do you mean, 'too perfect'?"

Danielle shrugs, "I don't know. They're all goody two-shoes," referring to the teenage characters featured in *Saved by the Bell*.

So the teacher responds, "That explains why you put it on the unreal side of the chart." Seeing Danielle's discomfort and not wanting to put her on the spot, the teacher turns to the class. "What do you think? Is *Saved by the Bell* more realistic than *Roseanne* and *Growing Pains*?"

Hands quickly rise in the air. One young man is critical, pointing out, "No way. They don't have a family. You never see those kids at home. No parents. They act like a family but they're just among friends. So, it's not nearly as realistic as *Roseanne* or *Growing Pains*."

A blond-haired young man counters this argument with his own analysis, saying:

> Even though these characters don't have parents like *Roseanne* and *Growing Pains* do, they still have real life issues that people are dealing with. And in *Growing Pains*, when those kids got problems, they go home and tell their parents. And everything is cool. But, in *Saved by the Bell*, they deal with their own problems on their own and some of the problems they face take more than one episode to resolve. That's makes this show more realistic than *Growing Pains*.

The class continues on, with various students coming to the board to explain their perceptions of the realism of shows including *Good Morning, America; The X-Files; A & E Biography; Montel Williams;* and *Judge Judy*. The more academically talented students give an impromptu presentation, with an attention-getting opening, a well-developed thesis statement with details and description, and a conclusion, while others have more trouble standing up to speak, verbalizing reasons with hesitation in this heterogeneous group. But even the shyest have made a minispeech in front of their peers in today's class, and while the smartest kids are leading the discussion, it also appears that the least academically inclined in the group are engaged—as I look around, there's no doodling, daydreaming, whispering, note passing, or heads on tables. As the teacher brings the class toward closure, she asks students to consider what broad themes or issues were identified in students' presentations as qualities that mark a TV show as realistic or unrealistic. As students call out ideas, they get written on the board.

Maria raises her hand. "A character that always acts the same way, under the same circumstances, is more stereotyped, less complex. That's less realistic. People are not stereotypes."

Robert says, "When stories are unpredictable, when you can't always tell what will happen, or how things will turn out, that's more realistic."

Probing students to reflect on the ideas developed as students talked about specific TV shows, the teacher says, "When you watch a TV show, perhaps even without thinking about it, you make a judgment about how realistic it is. What factors influence those judgments?" Kids respond.

"Sometimes the show claims to actually be real, like news or *A & E Biography*. And some dramas say, 'Based on a true story' and that makes you think it's real."

"Sometimes the show uses a shaky camera or grainy footage and it looks like home video, and that makes it seem more realistic, like *Cops*."

"Even when a show is totally fiction, like *The X-Files*, it can use a lot of sophisticated scientific stuff and that makes it seem realistic, like when they refer to technical and scientific stuff that you never heard of but it sounds important and true."

Sandra cautiously raises her hand, "When I was younger, I thought *Saved by the Bell* was realistic. To me, those kids seemed like real teenagers. Now that I'm older, I see how unrealistic it is. The actual show is the same. But I'm different now. So people think about realism differently depending on their life situation."

"How do we make these reality judgments?" the teacher asks. "Most of us compare the media message we see on the screen to what we already know. And we tend to believe media messages more when they match what we have previously experienced in real life." The teacher goes on to explain that she's never ridden in the back seat of a police car because she's never been arrested. But with so many media images of a police arrest rattling around in her memory from hundreds of TV shows and movies and books, she says that she feels like she knows what it looks like and feels like to be inside a police car. Because of her exposure to media's representations, she thinks that she would be able to distinguish a realistic arrest scene from an unrealistic arrest scene.

Devon pipes up, nearly interrupting the teacher, "So, with the cop car thing, you've seen it enough times on TV that when you see the same thing over and over again, you're going to think that the way they show it on TV is the way it really is. And then you end up surprised or angry when you find out that reality is not like they show it on TV."

Head lowered and eyes on the desk, another student, Shay, observes, "Even though movies and TV try to give you feelings about what something is like, you can't really know how you would feel, or how anybody else would feel, being in the back of that cop car."

The teacher probes, "You can't?"

"No," says Shay quietly. "It's scarier than they show on TV. It's a lot scarier."

The bell rings and the students pack up their notebooks and leave. The teacher has learned a lot about her students today because they have done most of the talking. She reflects on Shay's disclosure about his own experience in the back of a police car. She knows the comment was an eye-opener for some of the more affluent kids busy prepping for the SATs. She hopes her students have learned something about the complexity of reading the media, exploring media's complex and multidimensional representations of reality.

SEVEN YEARS LATER, the discussion about the nature of mediated reality continues at Concord High School. As "reality TV" has come to dominate the cultural landscape of television, with more than two dozen prime-time reality shows popular among adolescents, the discussion among English 11 students at Concord High School about the concept of *reality* has become richer, more nuanced, and more contested. The converging environments of television, the Internet, and new media are now enabling educators to engage with the semiotic challenges that Baudrillard (1994) has identified in his descriptions of how cultural symbols have detached from their relationship to the world. We live in a society that has become a cross-referential system of culturally constructed meanings, creating a funhouse of mirror-screens "each deflecting and yet projecting images and symbols of desire and identity onto human subjects" (Luke, 2003, p. 24). Growing up in such a culture, students are hungry for serious dialogue about what they experience via the mass media; when media content "becomes classroom subject matter, students' discussion and writing are not tentative" (Morris, 1989, p. 38). As students engage in sharing ideas and reflecting on experiences that matter to them, a learning environment is created where students can examine the relationships between meaning making, power, pleasure, and identity. As Postman (1985) has written, media literacy reflects the "acknowledged task of the schools to assist the young in interpreting the symbols of their culture" (p. 163). Whether we like it or not, media messages have shaped our understanding of many aspects of social reality. Even more powerful than our own life experiences, media texts are at the center of our cultural worlds.

MEDIA LITERACY IN ENGLISH LANGUAGE ARTS

Media literacy education in the context of English language arts has been highly influenced by the ongoing cross-disciplinary fertilization between the fields of communication, media studies, and literary and cultural studies. In the last 25 years postmodern theorists have been dismantling the high culture/low culture distinction, which has characterized the study of culture industries. They have emphasized how electronic imagery and digital media have become increasingly central to the development of globalization. As we move from an industrial to a postindustrial information economy, these scholars have argued for "broader definitions of knowledge, literacy and pedagogy which will include the study of the intertextuality of imageries, texts, icons and artifacts of new information economies, of media and of popular culture" (Luke, 2003, p. 27).

In the book, *The Rise and Fall of English*, Robert Scholes (1998) recommends a major overhaul in the teaching of English by replacing the canon of literary texts with a canon of concepts, precepts, and practices for investigating the meaning-making process. He suggests that restoring the medieval trivium of grammar, dialectic, and rhetoric as the center posts in English education will help students situate themselves in their own culture and make the basic processes of language and communication fully available for students' use.

When translated to K–12 education, this argument has helped to move media literacy from the periphery of the curriculum, where in some schools it had marginally existed as an elective course in journalism or film study, or sometimes was embedded within practical courses in video production. Scholes urges English educators to incorporate a wide range of texts including films, television, advertising, the Internet, music, and popular culture. With an ever-increasing range of media messages in so many forms, students need to understand the process by which authors convey meaning about socially constructed experience. The use of digital media and popular culture texts not only stimulates young people's engagement, motivation, and interest in learning, but enables them to build a richer, more nuanced understanding of how texts of all kinds work within a culture.

UNDERSTANDING "TEXTS" AND THE READING PROCESS

Recognizing the potential benefits of media literacy, the English teachers at Concord High School decided to design a new course for 11th-grade students that would build their understanding of the ways texts of all kinds work for readers and writers. They enlarged the definition of *texts* to include all the forms of symbolic expression that convey meaning from authors to readers. They recognized that media, technology, and popular culture present texts for people to interpret, actively or passively, and they sought ways to design learning experiences that would build what David Perkins has called *learning for understanding*. Understanding (as distinct from knowledge or skills) is a matter of being able to carry out a variety of performances—like making predictions about what would happen if there were a snowball fight in space. Generating predictions and making inferences demonstrate understanding and, at the same time, advance it by encompassing new situations. As Perkins

(1993) writes, "Most classroom activities are too routine to be understanding performances—spelling drills, true-and-false quizzes, arithmetic exercises, many conventional essay questions, and so on. Such performances have their importance too, of course. But they are not performances of understanding; hence they do not do much to build understanding" (p. 29). Perkins recommends that teachers make learning a long-term, thinking-centered process, providing for rich, ongoing assessment and guidance. He encourages teachers to use powerful representations and heuristic devices that help students build conceptual models and induct students into the discipline by showing them how people formulate and solve problems within a shared intellectual framework. Most important, he urges teachers to *teach for transfer*, helping students apply what they've learned in a variety of new contexts and encouraging them to see connections between ideas and information. Concord teachers believed that in helping students to engage actively with media texts in the classroom they could strengthen metacognitive strategies useful for a lifetime. In preparing students for life in the twenty-first century, they wanted students to become reflective and thoughtful and highly aware of the processes involved in accessing, analyzing, evaluating, composing, and communicating messages.

These ideas are well aligned with recent conceptualizations of the reading process (Kinzer & Leander, 2003; McLaughlin & DeVogel, 2004; Peters & Wixson, 2003; Rand Reading Study Group, 2004). Readers bring their cognitive abilities, motivation, prior knowledge, and life experiences to the process of reading. A specific print, digital, or visual text has features that influence the reading process as does the reading activity itself (whether one is viewing a TV show for entertainment, skimming the headlines of a newspaper, reading a novel for pleasure, or studying a textbook to prepare for a test). Concord teachers recognized that, in order to connect literacy to life, students needed to be able to apply a variety of effective strategies of meaning making in a range of different contexts and settings: at school or work, or for leisure or citizenship activities. They didn't just want to prepare students for taking tests in school; they wanted to prepare them for life in a highly complex, media-rich, and technologically dynamic cultural environment. English 11 teachers shared a real belief in empowerment, recognizing their role in producing meaningful social change by helping educate students. By starting from the premise that what these teachers did made a difference, this book aims to capture the complex kinds of learning that their students experienced.

A FOCUS ON CRITICAL QUESTIONS

The Concord High School course, English 11: Media/Communication, which debuted in fall 1998, integrated media literacy into English language

Figure 1.1. Using the Critical Questions to Analyze Media.

Choose a television show or event that you think is significant. Tape it. Watch it carefully. Ask yourself the five questions we've been considering this semester:

1. Who is sending the message and what is the author's purpose?
2. What techniques are used to attract and hold attention?
3. What lifestyles, values, and points of view are represented in this message?
4. How might different people interpret this message differently?
5. What is omitted from this message?

Watch the tape again. Decide which 10 minutes of the piece best represents what you think is significant about the program. Think about the questions again and answer them in five carefully written paragraphs. (15 points)

Bring the tape to class and be prepared to show it to the class and give a 3-minute presentation on its significance. (10 points)

You must submit your paragraphs on the date you do your presentation.

We'll pick names out of a hat to decide the order of presentations. If you are not prepared, you will receive a zero. If you don't have a VCR at home, speak to me. I'll tape your program for you, and we can arrange time for you to use my TV and VCR at school to prepare your presentation.

Source: Developed by Joanne McGlynn

arts. Seven teachers collaborated on the curriculum, in which students would analyze the language and images not only of traditional literary forms, but also websites, television shows, print and television journalism, films, advertising, political speeches, and business and interpersonal communications. To help unify their curriculum, the teachers adopted five critical questions that could be applied to any of the texts presented to students. Figure 1.1 shows the questions they had learned at the media literacy staff development program I offered at Clark University.

Teachers began the school year with critical viewing, writing, and discussion activities designed to showcase the power of these questions to strengthen analysis skills. For example, Joanne McGlynn would bring in taped examples of advertising, entertainment, and informational programming (from her ever-growing stockpile of videotaped episodes) and work through the process of involving students in exploring these questions. Sometimes she had students freewrite their responses, then read them aloud to share. Other times she asked small groups of students to work through the questions in discussion, making notes of the key ideas and sharing them as a large group afterwards. As Figure 1.1 shows, McGlynn developed an introductory writing and public speaking activity that made use of the critical questions and involved students in personally selecting a television program they perceived to be culturally significant. This activity helped McGlynn get to know her students as individuals, and the writing and speaking samples helped her assess the capacities and talents of each student as well as the areas of growth and improvement needed.

THE MEDIA LITERACY CURRICULUM AT CONCORD HIGH SCHOOL

The seven English 11 teachers had decided on some key focus themes for the Media/Communication course. These included:

- Advertising, persuasion, and propaganda
- The role of point of view in storytelling in dramatic film, television fiction, and contemporary and classic literature
- Humans' relationship with technology
- The role of journalism in society, including print, television news, and nonfiction genres
- The process of literary adaptation from literature to film
- Entertainment culture in historical context, including the role of global media corporations
- The representation of race, gender, and ideology in media messages
- The personal and social impact of media violence

In September 1998, the logistics of this new course were still largely unsolved and became a major focus of the planning, particularly as teachers had to decide how to allocate the limited access to teaching materials among the seven teachers. They purchased a number of sets of reading materials for students. Based on the themes they identified, they started with a class set of *Team Rodent* (1998), a critical commentary on the Disney Corporation and its social influence on American culture by Carl Hiassen. They also bought copies of a reflective book-length essay on the practice of journalism entitled *News Is a Verb* (1998) by veteran journalist Pete Hamill. They bought multiple subscriptions to *Brill's Content* magazine, a monthly publication developed by *American Lawyer* magazine and Court TV founder Steven Brill, which provided an in-depth look at the media business, including the worlds of publishing, television production, journalism, film, and news media. (The magazine was published from August 1998 to the fall of 2001.) They bought copies of Steven Stark's *Glued to the Set* (1997), a book of short essays about television history and cultural influence framed by a focus on thirty influential television programs from the 1950s *The Howdy Doody Show* to the 1990s *Roseanne*.

Among the works of classic and contemporary literature to be included in the Grade 11 curriculum were *Frankenstein* (1818/1994) by Mary Shelley, *As I Lay Dying* (1930/1957) by William Faulkner, *Beloved* (1987) by Toni Morrison, *One Flew Over the Cuckoo's Nest* (1962) by Ken Kesey, *Brave New World* (1946) by Aldous Huxley, and *1984* (1959) by George Orwell. The teachers created a plan so that all seven of them would have access to books and print materials for students at different points during the year. As a result, in mid-September some Grade 11 teachers were beginning the year with an introduction to the study of advertising, persuasion, and propaganda, while others were working on understanding and analyzing the news media. Still others were examining issues of representation and point of view in literature and contemporary media. Each teacher was charting a fresh course in this new terrain, even though some would start in September by reading classic literature and others would start with a focus on mass media. They had set up a local folder on the computer in the teachers' workroom to enable them to share materials for different topics. Although each teacher developed his or her own syllabus, lesson plans, and assignments, the general components of the units can be described as follows:

- *Journalism and information.* Students explored the process of learning to develop intellectual curiosity. They analyzed newscasts, including local, national, and newsmagazine broadcasts. They critically examined newspapers and websites, comparing coverage of an event or individual across multiple sources. They examined the process of remembrance, reflecting on how both literature and media messages shape our understanding of history by transmitting cultural understandings from one generation to the next. They studied communication techniques by analyzing word choice, images, sequence of information, content emphasis and omission, and patterns in racial and gender representation. They learned strategies for evaluating the credibility of information. They discussed the economic structure of the mass media, which emphasizes ratings and money as meaningful markers of quality.
- *Advertising, propaganda, and persuasion.* Students applied their ability to analyze messages by looking at television, advertising, and journalism. In analyzing advertising, students examined the techniques and approaches used in print and TV advertising. They determined target audiences and noted the use of emotional appeals and graphic design. Various students visited an advertising agency, taught a mini-unit on advertising to younger children, created ad parodies, or composed consumer awareness campaigns. They read Bradbury's *Farenheit 451*

(1967) and a young adult novel by M. T. Anderson, *Feed* (2002), a tragic romance/science fiction story about young people growing up in a culture where all their media comes to them from a chip implanted in their brains.

• *Representation of race, gender, and social class.* Students examined the concept of representation and reflected on the role of media and popular culture in shaping personal identity and an understanding of the social world. How do gender, race, age, and class shape our understanding of our own power or powerlessness? Whose voices are portrayed in the mass media and whose perspectives are omitted? What ideas and values are depicted in media representations? Students looked at changes in media representations of romance and dating from the 1950s to today by looking at patterns of relationships depicted in television programs from different time periods. They analyzed the issue of media violence by examining the role of conflict in storytelling, the impact of violent media on children and young people, and the function of media violence in maintaining cultural myths of power, independence, and freedom. They read *Glued to the Set* (Stark, 1997) to learn how specific shows reflected and shaped cultural values. They read Toni Morrison's *Beloved* (1987), a story with many voices that shows slavery as a paradigm of the complex power dynamics that exist in social relationships. They viewed Spike Lee's film, *Bamboozled* (2000), a satiric look at racism in American television that shows how America's racist past still impacts the present.

• *Storytelling.* Students explored the question: Who are our heroes? What is the relationship between the individual and the community? Students examined how point of view shapes the nature of a story. For example, students analyzed the point of view in Ken Kesey's book, *One Flew Over the Cuckoo's Nest* (1962), examining how the book and the film use different strategies to tell the story through manipulating point of view. They read *A Perfect Storm* (Junger, 1997) to discuss how the economics of the film blockbuster shape differences between storytelling in literature and film. Students analyzed Mary Shelley's *Frankenstein*, examining the different depictions of the birth of the monster in the many different film versions, from the 1931 *Frankenstein*, the 1974 *Young Frankenstein* parody, and the more recent film adaptation, *Mary Shelley's Frankenstein*. They got the chance to become storytellers themselves, writing screenplays to adapt Faulkner's *As I Lay Dying* (1930/1957) to create a film scene, composing creative fiction, examining storytelling structures used in film, and creating videos to capture their ideas using images, language, editing, and sound.

Another way of viewing English 11 is provided by Figure 1.2, which shows a prospectus created by Mike Robb Grieco for the course he offered in 2002–03. His diagram shows the themes he intended to explore during the school year, blending a description of questions, issues, and examples of books and films in a playful "advertisement" for the course.

RESEARCH METHODOLOGY

Since Concord High School began its English 11 media literacy curriculum in 1998, I have interviewed teachers, observed classrooms, and interviewed students in order to document teachers' approaches to implementing the curriculum. I also collected quantitative data to more closely examine student skill development over the course of one year and compare their performance to a matched control group. In writing this book, I made use of more than 700 pages of interview transcripts, 4 handwritten field notebooks, and nearly 200 different artifacts, including student writing, videos, lesson plans, and assignments. I gathered quantitative data from both Concord High School and a matched control group school to examine changes in students' interpretation of media texts, including print, visual, electronic, and audio formats. This research included 200 variables gathered from nearly 400 students at two points in time, for a total of nearly 16,000 data points. I used the research questions shown on Figure 1.3 to structure my inquiry. Throughout the process, I reflected on the actual activities and lessons that comprised the learning experiences, studied the way parents and school leaders interpreted the new approach to literacy, and examined the ways that teachers and students responded emotionally, socially, and intellectually to the experience of critically analyzing and composing using media texts, tools, and technologies.

As a result of the mixed-methods approach to this research, the overall portrait of English 11 at Concord High School includes both qualitative and quantitative accounts of the learning experience. American educational leaders have been struggling with the challenge of bringing the power of rigorous, scientific understanding to bear on improving decisions about education. There is tremendous controversy and lack of consensus about what it actually means for something to be based on "scientific research" in education (Bell, 2004; Flinders, 2003). In my research for this book I wanted to embrace both the particular and specific knowledge available to me through interviews and observations while at the same time seek to gather information that would permit broader generalizations about the utility of media literacy within the context of English language arts education. I rejected the arguments made by

Figure 1.2. Mike Robb Grieco's "Advertisement" for His English 11 Course.

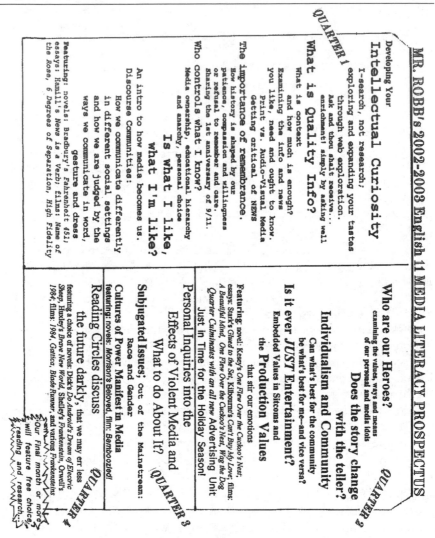

those scholars who impose strict definitions of what should and should not be counted as scientific or establish a hierarchy of methods based on competing accounts of social theory. Instead, I preferred to use qualitative methods to understand the contextual details of local practice at Concord High School and quantitative methods as a means to generate a better understanding of the

Figure 1.3. Guiding Research Questions of This Book.

Teacher Focus

- What motivates teachers' interest in media literacy instruction?
- What existing teacher attitudes, skills, knowledge, and behaviors lead to "best practices" in media literacy instruction?

Program Focus

- What types of media literacy instruction do teachers most commonly employ?
- How does media literacy instruction vary over time?
- How do teachers use media literacy materials and resources?
- What topics or issues are more frequently explored by teachers and students?
- How does media literacy instruction affect instruction in other skills and subject areas?
- What are "best practices" in media literacy instruction?

Community Focus

- How do parents and community leaders respond to media literacy instruction?
- How to colleagues and school administrators respond?

Student Focus

- How do students respond to media literacy instruction?
- Does media literacy improve students' literacy skills?
- Does media literacy alter students' attitudes about school?
- Does media literacy affect motivation, confidence, or aspects of identity development?
- Does media literacy affect quality of relationship between teacher and student?
- Do media literacy lessons from the classroom transfer to nonschool settings?

---

program's impact on student performances, attitudes, behaviors, and literacy practices. Readers can find more technical information about the research design, sampling, and statistical analysis in the Appendix.

THE ORGANIZATION OF THIS BOOK

Concord High School is one of the first school districts in the United States to integrate media literacy so extensively in the secondary curriculum.

This book examines their comprehensive approach to incorporating media literacy in English language arts through interviews with high school teachers who collaborated on the development of the curriculum. Readers get a close look at some of the books, films, and classroom activities that were used (see the list of resources at the end of the book for more information). The outcomes of this instruction on students' writing, reading, listening, and viewing skills in responding to TV news, advertising, and print media are then presented. The teachers at Concord High School were pioneers and trailblazers: they had not had much prior knowledge or training in media literacy. When they began in 1998, they didn't feel completely confident about what they were doing. Nine years later, they have a much clearer sense of the focus of the course and its educational objectives, but are still challenged on how to continue to make the course relevant and meaningful to students in a continually transforming media environment. This book uncovers what teachers experienced in trying to implement this new curriculum and what their students actually learned.

Chapter 2 provides a close look at the institutional context that led the English faculty at Concord High School to expand the concept of literacy. They needed district approval of a new course for 11th graders as part of the required curriculum for all students in the district. How did they gain support from colleagues within the English Department, the school administration, and the School Committee? What were the concerns of the principal, other English teachers, and parents? What structural factors and institutional values helped support the decision to implement this new curriculum?

In Part II, Teaching Media Literacy, readers get a detailed look at what happened in the English 11 classrooms at Concord High School. Chapter 3 explores the ways that English 11 teachers used the question, "Who is telling the story?" to build critical thinking skills in the classroom, explore issues of objectivity, bias, and point of view, and examine storytelling structures in news and fiction. Chapter 4 examines the curriculum's emphasis on advertising, persuasion, and propaganda, reviewing how teachers organized the scope of instruction to examine concepts like branding, target audience, and the role of consumption in our cultural environment. Teachers wove together more traditional literary analysis activities with the study of media genres to generate many different writing activities involving screenwriting and historical analysis. Chapter 5 shows how teachers tackled the topic of representation, those "pictures of the world inside our heads," a phrase used first by Walter Lippmann (1922) to describe the function of stereotypes for citizens in a democracy, who must rely on images and information presented to them by political elites. English 11 teachers explored patterns of gender and racial representation, the representation of mental illness and even the depiction of the "monster" in literature and film.

In Part III, Measuring Media Literacy, readers learn about the impact of the curriculum on students' critical thinking, viewing, listening, reading, analysis, and citizenship skills. Chapter 6 shows how students learned "to read the word and the world," as Freire and Macedo (1987) explain how literacy is preceded by and intertwined with knowledge of the world and action in response to it. In the politically active community of Concord, New Hampshire, students at Concord High School got a small chance to shape the political discourse of the 2000 presidential campaign, learning a lot in the process about the routines and meta-narratives of daily journalism. By devising a way of operationalizing the concept of "analyzing media messages," I found some important evidence of growth in students' ability to comprehend and analyze television and radio news and commentary.

Chapter 7 reports on data collected to measure students' ability to analyze advertising. Evidence from this study shows that, compared to the control group, students strengthened their ability to understand that advertising is generally targeted to a highly specific group of consumers, that many different verbal and visual techniques are used to attract attention and increase viewer involvement in advertising, and that the purpose of advertising is often to create an emotional association between the product and a desirable feeling or state of mind. Framed by an examination of the scholarly literature on young people and advertising, this chapter demonstrates how the analysis of media texts in the classroom can enhance critical thinking about message purpose, design, and point of view.

Chapter 8 provides evidence concerning the impact of the English 11 curriculum on students' reading comprehension, analysis, and writing skills. By looking closely at the experience of students enrolled in the program as compared to a matched control group, I found improvements in students' ability to summarize a nonfiction text and analyze rhetorical techniques used in print. Students themselves reflect on their learning experiences and explain how their reading, writing, and media consumption practices have been transformed.

The Conclusion reviews the major findings of the research presented in the book, examining the contribution of the learning environment to the English 11 curriculum, including school structure, administrative leadership, and community values. It also explores the role of teachers' political beliefs in the teaching of media literacy. The impact of media literacy on educational policy in English language arts is examined, reflecting on the ways that media literacy educators respond to the opportunities and challenges posed by the Internet and other digital technologies.

Information, entertainment, and knowledge are undergoing a historical transformation, and the social consequences of the technological innovations surrounding communications media are complex. Teachers at Concord High School took a bold and courageous step in designing the English 11 Media/ Communication course. They adapted instructional methods in secondary language arts education to meet the needs of students in contemporary society. It is hoped that this book may encourage others to explore the pathways they pioneered.

Chapter 2

An Opportunity to Expand
the Concept of Literacy

It was September 1998, and seven English teachers at Concord High School were beginning their new course, English 11, with a plan for a yearlong focus on media/communication. "We don't have the security of having had a year under our belt," said Bob Cowan in describing the general anxiety of the teaching team in spite of their summer planning.

This chapter examines the circumstances that enabled the English teachers at Concord High School to integrate media literacy into the curriculum. It shows how school administrators and faculty colleagues responded to the new ideas about using television, advertising, films, and popular culture as texts in the classroom, and examines how parents and community members provided feedback during the first years of the program's implementation.

THE COMMUNITY

As the capital city of New Hampshire, the city of Concord has a proud tradition of excellence in public education. With a population of 42,000 residents, the community is relatively homogeneous with a largely White population of skilled and semiskilled workers, but is experiencing a rise in its minority population that adds greater cultural and ethnic diversity. The median household income in 2003 ranged from $32,733 to $39,531 with only 6.7% of the families in the school district having incomes below the poverty level. Concord's expenditure per pupil is $6,864, slightly higher than New Hampshire's average of $6,611, with about half the money coming from state funding and the rest through local funding. During the 2005–06 school year, the high school enrolled 1,962 students.

CONCORD HIGH SCHOOL

The mission statement of Concord High School says, "Our community of learners will challenge and expect its members to realize their highest potential. Our community will create a positive learning environment through mutual respect and effective communication." Educators aim to provide challenging curriculum and learning experiences and expect students to be able to use knowledge of the cultural and natural world based on an evolving core of concepts and information. The mission emphasizes students' roles as:

- *Active self-directed learners,* who inquire creatively about their world, take risks, and examine options as they initiate actions and complete tasks
- *Effective communicators,* who write well, read widely and in depth, listen perceptively, share ideas orally, and use language, numbers, and symbols to convey and receive information
- *Effective collaborators,* who assume various roles to accomplish group or community goals, using self-knowledge, compromise, cooperation, and respect
- *Informed decision makers,* who define the issue, research alternatives, consider consequences, and make choices that demonstrate intellectual integrity and rigorous evaluation
- *Creative producers* of art in the classical, contemporary, and practical traditions using invention, design, and critical assessment
- *Life planners,* who determine options and pursue career and personal goals including a consideration for physical, emotional, and mental well-being
- *Community participants,* who understand and practice democratic traditions and values, including respect for human dignity, honesty, and fairness, and who accept the consequence of their actions

The Concord High School mission statement emphasizes the importance of establishing reasonable and challenging expectations; using civil, non-violent methods of communicating differences and resolving conflict; respecting and protecting individual differences, roles, responsibilities, and contributions; practicing a positive work ethic, using all avenues of communication while valuing face-to-face personal interaction; and celebrating positive performance.

Students

Concord High School students have demonstrated strength in English language arts. Evidence from the New Hampshire State assessments, the New Hampshire Educational Improvement and Assessment Program (NHEIAP), shows that students are performing well in reading comprehension, analysis, and writing skills. Data from the 2002–03 school year reveal that Concord High School students were performing better than the state average on the end of Grade 10 English examination. The assessment instruments are based on New Hampshire curriculum frameworks that were cooperatively developed by educators at all levels, business people, government officials, community representatives, and parents. This test includes elements where students read a short passage and demonstrate their understanding through completing multiple-choice questions. Open-response questions ask students to write a paragraph that explains their level of understanding or to solve a problem and explain their reasoning. In addition, students are asked to demonstrate their ability to communicate in writing by composing an extended essay in response to a writing assignment. During the 2002–03 school year, Concord students performed above average compared to state averages. For example, 12% of Concord Grade 10 students scored at the advanced level compared to only 7% statewide; 36% scored at the proficient level compared to 26% statewide. These data show that Concord High School has a high-functioning program in English language arts.

The number of dropouts has been on the decline since the 2002–03 school year. State data show that nearly 5% of students dropped out of high school annually in the early 2000s, amounting to a cumulative dropout rate of 16–18%. The annual dropout rate is the percentage of students that drop out during a one-year period. The cumulative rate is an estimate of the percentage of high school students who will not graduate. By 2003, the number of dropouts was reduced to around 3% of the population annually, for a cumulative dropout rate of about 13%. Many factors may contribute to changes in the dropout rate, but it's impossible to evaluate the impact of the English 11 Media/Communication course on the annual student dropout rate because, beginning in 2000–01, the dropout counts and rates are not comparable with counts and rates published for past years. The definition of a dropout has changed significantly and the formula for calculating the rate is different. Overall, Concord's dropout rate has nearly exactly paralleled the state averages (New Hampshire Department of Education, 2005).

With two thirds of the class of 2002 intending to pursue some form of higher education and the rest headed for the workforce or the military, Concord High School, although not as racially diverse as the rest of the nation, is not so different from many public secondary schools across the United States.

Teachers

The Concord community is proud of their most famous teacher, Christa McAuliffe, the first teacher in space, who died tragically in the explosion of the space shuttle Challenger on January 28, 1986. In 1982, McAuliffe accepted a position to teach in the Social Studies Department at Concord High School. It was here that she developed the curriculum for a course called The American Woman. The course explored the history of the United States from the female perspective and relied heavily upon the journals and letters of the women who lived it. It was at Concord High School that McAuliffe's reputation as an exuberant and creative teacher first began to grow. Her motto "I touch the future—I teach" reflects the deep sense of social responsibility that many teachers at Concord High School share.

School administrators seem genuinely proud of their faculty. Most of the teachers at Concord High School have a college major in their teaching area and about 50% of the faculty have a master's degree. In 2004–05, the average teacher salary in the district was $50,491 with a starting salary minimum of $30,724. The average teacher-student ratio is 1:21 with 6 hours and 30 minutes of instructional time per day. Teachers at Concord High School point to how their core values are enacted through day-to-day collaborative decision making and respect between school administrators, faculty, staff, students, and parents. And the teachers sense the high expectations, which affect their own performance in the classroom as well. "It's a challenging, stimulating, and wonderful place to work" was a refrain I heard often during my visits at Concord High School.

Facilities

Concord High School's complex of buildings includes a skillful mix of old and new, situated just outside the town center in a densely populated residential district and nearby one can find the many administrative buildings of the state capital. The distinguished granite columns of the old school, built in 1927, face the street, with more modern additions, housing a gymnasium, cafeteria, and shop wing, constructed in the 1960s. In 1980 the school underwent major renovations with the addition of a new vocational wing. This wing, now called the Concord Regional Technology Center at Concord High School, serves 550 students from 29 towns in the region. During the 1995–96 school year faculty and students remained in the building while Concord High School began a $23-million addition and renovation, adding a large modern building connected to the original school by a glass skywalk. The Concord High campus now sports a new library/media center located at the center of the school, a student center and cafeteria, and a performing arts area. Using the small-schools model, Concord High School has four commons areas, which divides students into four learning communities (by alphabetical order). Each commons has its own administrative and student community, creating a more personal sense of community within this large high school. Within each commons area are lockers, an assistant principal, guidance counselors, learning specialists, and support staff.

When cable television arrived in Concord in the mid-1980s, the cable company established a small, local access facility at Concord High School. Concord AT&T, formerly Media One, the cable company, has been in a continual tug-of-war with the town's political leaders for a number of years. Concord is one of the more than 2,000 communities that established a community television access center as part of the franchise agreement with the cable company. Like many communities, there is tension between the cable company and the town about the level of services to be provided, particularly in terms of program staffing. Even though the local access center is located in the high school, only students enrolled in the one elective course in television production are authorized to use the community access facilities because of personnel limitations. As a result, Concord High School has a television production center but cannot fully control it. Students do not have access to the kinds of TV production studios seen in many high schools of comparable size and there is only very limited access to video cameras and editing equipment.

DISTRICT GROWTH AND OPPORTUNITIES FOR CHANGE

The decision to expand Concord High School helped to alleviate some of the overcrowding at the district's middle schools and created an opportunity for curricular revision. When the school was being enlarged, English teachers began preparing for the Grade 9 students who, for the first time, would soon be enrolled in the high school. As teacher Val Aubry explained:

Because Concord High had always been a 3-year high school, we needed to make some changes to the overall program. We learned that our 10th-grade curriculum had rather closely mirrored the 9th-grade curriculum at the middle school since, as you might expect, there was very little communication between the middle schools and the high school. So, it was a complicated decision, but one which we've said: let's change it all. If we're going to change, let's really change. And let's try to work something out so we can do something interdisciplinary with social studies.

The newly created Grade 9 curriculum, which the English faculty had developed, made effective use of cross-disciplinary teaming. Students were heterogeneously grouped in English, social studies, and biology. In order to best support the team approach to teaching Grade 9, the English Department reviewed the curriculum and made the decision to focus the course on world literature since the focus of the Grade 9 social studies course was world history. The Grade 9 teachers actively sought ways to maximize the potential connections across the subject areas. As Aubry describes it, "It was astoundingly hard work, but very fulfilling. We collaborated to create an unusual curriculum

of contemporary world literature that is somewhat accessible to freshmen."
As chairperson of the Grade 9 curriculum committee, Aubry was exhausted
by the work involved in creating this new course, and so she didn't chime in
as fast to work on the Grade 11 Media/Communication course. Based on
her previous experience, she was able to anticipate how much hard work and
preparation would be involved.

Block Scheduling

After careful reflection and considerable debate, block scheduling was
established at Concord High School in 1996. There are four 90-minute
blocks of time per day to allow flexibility for a diversity of instructional
activities. At Concord, students have English every other day. The
scheduling change was linked to an interest in decreasing the amount of
standard lecture-discussion-seatwork type of instruction. Teachers were
interested in increasing opportunities to individualize instruction and use
creative teaching strategies. Larger blocks of time do allow for a more flexible
and productive classroom environment, along with more opportunities for
using varied and interactive teaching methods. Other benefits include more
effective use of school time, decreased class size, increased number of course
offerings, reduced numbers of students with whom teachers have daily
contact, and the ability of teachers to use more process-oriented strategies.
These elements turned out to be essential for the learning activities at the
heart of the English 11 curriculum, which required sustained time for small-
group and large-group discussion and hands-on activities as well as time for
reading, viewing, and writing.

Heterogeneous Grouping

Concord High School's English Department has used heterogeneous
grouping since the 1980s, even though the Social Studies and Science
Departments in the high school do not mix students heterogeneously but
instead track students by ability after Grade 9. Heterogeneous grouping—
mixing students of different ability levels in academic classes (instead of offering
distinct courses of varying levels of challenge)—is an approach sometimes
used in secondary education when teachers attempt to set higher goals for
students, like developing critical thinking and independent learning, in order
to maximize learning opportunities for all students (Cushman, 1992).

Legal challenges to tracking have pointed out that ability grouping tends to
segregate students by race and social class as substantially higher percentages
of African American, Hispanic, and low-income students are placed in lower
track courses (Loveless, 1999; Lucas, 1999; Walberg, Reynolds, & Wang,

2004). Tracking itself takes different forms at different schools, with some schools labeling courses with names like "honors," "college prep," "general ed," or "special ed."

Many Concord High School English teachers believe that heterogeneous grouping helps all students, the high-achieving college-bound student as well as the student who is headed to trade school or the workplace. Some are familiar with the literature, which shows no statistically significant differences in student achievement on standardized tests between tracked and untracked students (Lucas, 1999). Some have experienced how students who are tracked have lower expectations of themselves, which affects their classroom performance. Teachers at Concord High School, like advocates of mixed-ability grouping across the United States, argue that when authentic assessment is used, teachers can actually set higher standards for all students. Rather than watering down academic standards, heterogeneous grouping helps raise standards, even for the highest achieving students, and helps create a school culture where intellectual energy is the rule rather than the exception (Sizer, 1996). Many Concord teachers in the English department believe that mixed-ability grouping not only affects academic skills, but carries over into classroom behavior as well, encouraging civility and respect for diversity among students who grow to appreciate the unique array of talents and life experiences in their classrooms, school, and community.

Some opposition to heterogeneous grouping has come from the parents of high-achieving students, who fear classes have become less challenging as they accommodate the learning needs of those less well prepared. But most respect the views of teachers like Bob Cowan, who remembers the discussions about heterogeneous grouping that occurred in the English Department. He recalls being the only one to vote against the decision and noted, "Since that time, many moons ago, I have become a convert because I think we have made such terrific gains in terms of how kids see themselves in relation to other kids and their own abilities." He acknowledged that the move to heterogeneous grouping has required the use of instructional methods that take advantage of collaborative learning, project-based curricula, and seminar-style discussions. "Whatever might be lost in terms of a traditional approach to curriculum where the teacher did all the talking—that kind of purveying of content isn't as meaningful or lasting as some of the dynamics that we can set up within student-centered teams which have kids with diverse points of view," Cowan explained. "We routinely get whole-class discussions where a large number of students participate."

Similarly, English 11 teacher Val Aubry found heterogeneous grouping deeply satisfying even though she acknowledges the challenges associated with meeting the needs of students with diverse abilities in a single class-room:

For me this matches my philosophy on some kind of a deep level. I believe that every kid in this country deserves access to a really good education. And I taught low-level kids for years. And I love them. They're who I went into teaching for. But I no longer believe that isolating them in a trap where I wrote for them, I read to them, I gave them their pencil and loved them intensely is the best thing I can do for them.

Students were also aware of how heterogeneous grouping affected the classroom. They commented on the wide range of attitudes and perspectives among their peers in responding to the literature and media that were read in the course. Many students described the quality of discussions in small groups, remembering situations when they found it valuable to share ideas about the readings and class activities with others. One explained, "When you did understand it, you could explain it to other people, and when you didn't, they could explain it to you." But one student told me that the variety of learning styles in the class made it challenging because some students were comfortable with the reading because they were able to comprehend the work and others were frustrated by it and felt that the reading was a chore. Sometimes this affected the ability of small groups to be effective, resulting in groups where one student did all the work, leaving the others to be passive. As another student described it, "We were just kind of stuck [because we didn't do the reading] and we had to, you know, 'yes' our way through."

Heterogeneous grouping has a flip side, of course. A number of kids at Concord High School now fail English courses because the expectations for all students are high—there is no "dummy track" for the students with weaker abilities. From 2003 to 2005, approximately 10% of the student population was retained from grade promotion. Heterogeneous grouping continues to be controversial within the building. Muttering has occasionally been heard among some guidance counselors, science and math faculty, and even some students. For example, the English Department does not offer any Advanced Placement classes, and some students and parents are angry about that. The high-stakes testing fever has reached New Hampshire and made parents fearful that their children will not be competitive in the increasingly ferocious drive to get into the best colleges. In helping to educate parents, the faculty decided to take a risk last spring, and they paid half the testing costs for ten randomly selected seniors to take the AP English exam. Three students got the highest score of 5, and three others received a 4, three got a 3, and one student got a 2, despite not having taken a course explicitly labeled "Advanced Placement." The English Department's success with heterogeneous grouping probably was a factor that influenced faculty confidence in moving to incorporate media literacy into the curriculum.

But the English Department has recognized that some students may desire the opportunity to do more sophisticated work, and so within each English class, teachers offer "challenge" assignments for students who elect to do additional work. For each unit, teachers invite students to sign up for the "challenge" assignment, and these students are given additional readings, homework, and course assignments. The work these students do is integrated into the regular classroom, which the teachers say has a beneficial effect on all students in the classroom.

For Grade 12 students, the department has long offered students a wide range of electives that are open to student choice, including film study, public speaking, poetry, drama, television production, and creative writing. Most faculty were satisfied with this approach, as it enabled academically talented students to take more than one English class in the upper grades. Courses in British literature and Shakespeare, according to Cowan, amount to a kind of de facto tracking situation as only a small number of the most academically talented students choose these courses.

ENGLISH 11 BECOMES "MEDIA/COMMUNICATION"

After consulting with the social studies faculty, the English Department decided to move the American Literature course from Grade 11 to Grade 10, where it would be well aligned with the required social studies course in American History. In Grades 11 and 12, students take elective courses in the Social Studies Department, and so the English Department had more freedom to imagine how to focus the curriculum for Grade 11. For the required yearlong Grade 11 course in English, the faculty thought long and hard about a possible year of English literature, with a focus on British authors. And there were some traditionalists among them who felt that was the way to go. In recalling the faculty discussions during the 1997–98 school year, Val Aubry said,

> Several people began to talk about the issue of relevance. And was it time for us to really face up to the fact that we were not here to make kids potential English majors. Instead, we were aiming to help students become critical thinkers in responding to the world they live in. And that was when we made this huge leap toward media literacy for English 11. We imagined a course called "Media/Communication" that would address nonfiction reading and writing, explore issues of media influence, examine advertising from a critical perspective, reflect and analyze visual approaches to the narrative, and encourage students to "read" the media of their everyday life with a critical eye. And when we voted, I think it was unanimous.

But at least one faculty member had a change of heart during the drive home after that meeting. As Aubry recalled, "The next day, a colleague called for another meeting and said, 'I'm not comfortable. I think we made a wrong move.'" The vote was taken again, and only one faculty member cast a dissenting vote. The faculty talked about the importance of moving toward consensus and began to realize that now they had to turn the idea into a reality. In Part II, I provide an overview of the curriculum that teachers developed as they invented the brand-new English 11 course.

Support from School Leaders

Principal Tim Mayes was pleased when he arrived at Concord High School in the fall of 1998 to discover that the English Department had just revised the English 9 curriculum and were launching a revision of English 11 during the 1998–99 school year. "My perception is that the world of kids today is different from that of 20 years ago and that our curriculum needs to be aligned with the needs of the students we teach. Our society is changing and basically it's a media-oriented world. We need to prepare kids for it," he said.

In the spring of 1998, the English faculty had made a presentation to the instructional committee of the school board and also to the full board. As Principal Mayes described it, the board is progressive on matters of curriculum and instruction, and they responded positively to the suggested changes to the curriculum. "They had only one concern: don't lose the academic rigor. Don't lose the emphasis on some of the basic skills that kids need: reading, writing, and interpreting literature, and that kind of thing," Mayes recalled. When Beth York, head of the English department, and her English 11 colleagues described their plan to incorporate literature and media into a rich curriculum that emphasized critical analysis, reading, writing, speaking, and seminar-style discussions, the school board members were enthusiastic.

Colleagues Respond to the New Curriculum

Some of the instructional staff at Concord High School have been key supporters of the English Department's decision to create English 11. According to many English teachers, the library media specialist has responded wonderfully to this course. "She is just throwing materials at us," said one. "And she is buying tons of new magazines. And she's really helping students and faculty." Christine Oskar-Poisson felt well supported by her colleagues at Concord High, noting that there is a climate of mutual respect at the school. However, that climate of mutual respect plus the high expectations for individual teacher performance may also have helped to create a live-and-let-live approach to cross-disciplinary connections within the school. Oskar-Poisson was one of the few teachers to describe a specific consultation with a teacher in the Social Studies department. She was doing her unit on advertising, persuasion, and propaganda, and the economics teacher was doing a unit on advertising at the same time. A student pointed out the connection, and so Oskar-Poisson and the economics teacher met and discussed their different approaches and designed the lessons in a complementary way. But this was a rare experience.

Formal interdepartmental meetings seldom occur at Concord High School. Each year, when I asked about cross-departmental collaboration between English and Social Studies faculty, a number of English 11 teachers told me in interviews of their interest in getting together with their colleagues in the Social Studies department to explore potential opportunities for collaboration. But year after year, time passed without much evidence of coordination. The live-and-let-live approach even limited the level of collaboration within members of the department. Jon Kelly, the Concord English teacher who taught the Television Production course, routinely offered to help his colleagues learn the rudiments of video production so that they could include exercises and activities in English 11, but teachers were too busy and preoccupied with their own exciting new work to collaborate. When the visiting team of the New England Association of Schools and Colleges came to evaluate the district, this lack of interdisciplinary collaboration was noted as a key weakness (Pederson, Golden, & Connolly, 2003).

But active community engagement by the English 11 faculty did play out in some aspects of administrative decision making. When a Concord vice principal led the charge to install televisions in the student center cafeteria, some of the English 11 teachers objected. These televisions were continually on in the lunch area, set to PBS, CNN, and MSNBC among others. When the many incidents of school shooting followed the tragic episode at Columbine High School in Littleton, Colorado, English 11 teacher Bob Cowan led the opposition, asking the principal, "Is this what we want school to, in effect, endorse, in terms of media consumption?" So the principal decided to bring the question of having televisions in the school cafeteria before the school senate, and Cowan went to offer his testimony in opposition. In the end, after much discussion and debate, students voted to keep the televisions in the cafeteria, and school administrators demonstrated respect for students' views, even in the face of faculty opposition.

Inside the English department, people have been uniformly supportive of those teachers who took leadership for creating English 11. According to Joanne McGlynn, there was some real reticence that the course would be too topical. Teachers wondered about the consequences of relying on media "texts" that would change each year and wondered if there would be any content that could exist year after year. When teachers shared all the materials they developed with their colleagues to launch the program, their colleagues were impressed and delighted. McGlynn glowed when she described the reaction of her senior colleague, a veteran teacher, whose response to the new course was, "It is simply impressive."

Beth York was prepared for more flak from her departmental colleagues when they first launched the program. She recalled, "In the beginning, some were uncomfortable, and I remember people talking about whether we had to hire people who had special qualifications to teach English 11." But now that colleagues have seen the curriculum and understood its purpose, the faculty is uniformly supportive. According to York, "People respect our passion for this work, and certainly some of the folks who are more of the traditional bent have really come around to it."

Parent and Community Response

In early September 1998, only a small number of Grade 11 parents showed up for Parent's Night, but none of the faculty were surprised. Only the Grade 9 parents were out in force, happy to be visiting their children's new school. By high school, most parents rely on information from their children, and many attend events directed at their youngest children, not their high schoolers. But Bob Cowan reported that some of the parents who did come to Parent's Night stayed after the session to tell him that the course was a great idea. He recalled, "One woman who I thought was going to hit me with a 2 x 4, who was very stone-faced through the whole thing, stayed an extra 15 minutes to get her chance." This parent was hosting a German exchange student. She said, "This is the most wonderful thing. I think it's a great direction to be going in." She appreciated that "there is a huge chunk of literature still in the course" and told Cowan that the books are more likely to be inherently interesting because of the way that the themes connect with the examination of media's influence and role in society. "Teenagers will have something to say in this class," she added.

By mid-November, however, when parents participated in individual conferences, a number of parents were pleased to report on what was different about life at home. Tareah Gray, a student teacher, described the reaction she received from many parents, who told her, "We are talking about all this stuff at home. My child is so excited about this class!" One of Gray's students shared her course materials with her father, and the father reported that he and his daughter now look at that sheet as they watch television together.

Val Aubry was pleased to learn at parent conferences in November that her students were talking about the course at home. Several parents spoke about the quality of family communication in response to some topic or idea related to media, technology, and society. She pointed out that "these are kids who are not the top students in the class, not the ones you would have thought that their parents would say they're chatting about what happens at school." Aubry said she wouldn't have been surprised to hear that her best students were talking to their parents about the ideas, themes, and topics of the course. But the parents who told her of their children's interest in the course were students who were the "midrange kind of kids who maybe conceptually have a little bit more difficulty with English class." Repeatedly over the years, Aubry had parents tell her, "My child really likes this course." Most English 11 teachers echoed this sentiment, saying that they had heard supportive comments from many parents. According to James Doneski, "Parents were blown away that their kids liked it."

Because media literacy is a practice that connects the school to the home (where most media consumption takes place), improvements in parent–teen communication patterns may have significant positive effects on adolescent development. Many parents complain that the quality of communication with their child diminishes during the teenage years, as young people associate more with their peers. Developmental psychologists have used attachment theory to examine family communication practices, finding that when teens have stronger attachments to parents, it gives them a sense of security that promotes independence in school and social settings. Attachment to parents during the teen years serves to simultaneously protect teens from the more stressful aspects of adolescence while helping them develop the confidence to explore new tasks and new environments (Larose & Boivin, 1998).

The possibility that media literacy in school may be associated with the quality of parent–child interaction has been proposed by scholars who research *parental mediation,* or the role of parents in the media consumption process. For example, in a study of how parents talk with their children about body image representations on television, data revealed that parental mediation of this incidental content—even if it criticized the television images—encouraged deep processing of the images (Nathanson & Botta, 2003). However, despite general agreement about the value of parental intervention, there is much less evidence that it happens in practice. It may simply be that parents are too busy to intervene in their children's media consumption experiences. Because parents are also much less likely to regulate their children's viewing as they reach adolescence, the accounts of increased active family communication among parents and their teens at Concord High School are noteworthy. The question about the potential impact of media literacy on family communication is a topic that deserves further study.

Of course, not every parent was enthusiastic. A few were concerned about the values messages in the course. Val Aubry explained:

> I had a mother, who's very religious, concerned about Huxley's *Brave New World,* come in and say, "Why are you teaching these messages?" And I had to explain why we were trying to teach them to be more aware of the messages they get outside of the home. She was very concerned

about teaching values here. It was a wonderful conversation, I think, for both of us. And her son—it was interesting—because I think just having that reassurance from home has helped his performance, now that his mother has a deeper understanding why we're doing what we're doing.

During the first months that English 11 rolled out in the fall of 1998, a small group of students and parents shared their fears and concerns with English 11 teachers. According to Tareah Gray, "I met with one set of parents who are very religious and they're antimedia. They don't have a TV in their house at all. Their son is displeased with the course, saying, 'I'm supposed to learn television. I don't even watch television. I'm not allowed to watch television.'" Gray didn't know exactly how to handle this student, whose lack of motivation and poor focus resulted in numerous assignments that were missing or incomplete. "He comes into class negative all the time. I've had to kick him out a couple of times and call the parents. And they're frustrated with him, because he has an anger management problem anyway. But the parents respond, 'Well, we don't really see why he needs to be reading books this hard. And why does he need to be learning about TV? We don't even own a TV.'" Gray has done her best to explain why the course is important, and she can see that the parents are being polite in interacting with her, but she wonders if they understand even the basic concept of why it's important to learn to critically analyze media messages.

Surprisingly, some parents who worked in media professions were unsupportive. Christine Oskar-Poisson had a student whose parent had worked as a journalist. When he visited her class, he explained that he doesn't think that it's all that beneficial for people to be learning about the media in high school. He had concerns that the course was building cynicism by not presenting the work of journalists with an appropriate level of respect. Oskar-Poisson got the impression that his daughter was reflecting back the negative attitudes about the course that she was hearing at home. In an interview, this student said:

> My dad and his girlfriend both used to be TV journalists, and they were all upset when they found out that we were being taught to be so suspicious of the news. Questions like "What is omitted from this message?" As if the media were trying to control your brain! My dad said, "That's not really how it works. Sometimes you can't help putting your personal biases into the work that you do." My dad was trained to not be biased. And saying that he doesn't know to not be biased is insulting to him.

This perspective reflects a reaction that media professionals sometimes experience when they learn about media literacy. It's a posture of defensiveness that comes from the fear that media literacy fosters cynicism.

On the other hand, many professional journalists do see value in teaching kids to be media literate. Such courses are vital, says veteran network correspondent Marvin Kalb, a senior fellow at the Joan Shorenstein Center for the Press, Politics, and Public Policy at Harvard University's John F. Kennedy School of Government. "It has always been my belief since the Shorenstein Center started in 1987 that we needed to get young people to understand what they see and read in journalism," he says. "In a free and open society, there is a tremendous amount of information—the question is how to make sense of it." He adds, "It is also clear that [an understanding of] journalistic practices—the way journalists write, the way they present news—is drifting away from young people and therefore from American society" (Tugend, 2003, March, p. 1).

A few parents felt that the focus of the course was too political and that English should be a respite from the complex world of ideological values, particularly those that explored social injustice and racism. One particular student was in another teacher's English 11 section for a few weeks when there was a personality conflict; the assistant principal, at the parent's request, removed him and put him into Joanne McGlynn's class. When the parent first contacted McGlynn, the parent's dispute concerned the literature used in English 11. The parent did not want her son to read *Beloved* by Toni Morrison, so McGlynn assigned an alternate book. But when the student stopped doing his work, McGlynn called the parent twice. The parent turned the problem away from her son's performance and toward the content of English 11, saying, "Well, I have to tell you, I've been talking to parents and students and there's lots of unhappiness with the course. We feel that this course is not appropriate." She has a daughter who is in another English 11 class with another teacher. And when McGlynn asked for more information, the parent responded, "I feel as though the course is simply too political. They are inundated with images in the media all the time. To have them focus even more on it in an English class seems like overkill." When parents voiced their concerns about the course's exploration of the news media, teachers generally felt well supported by the school administration. McGlynn was sanguine about the feedback about the course: "One of my friends the other night said, 'You know, Joanne, when someone says, complains about something being too political, it is often because they don't share your politics.'"

THE ENERGIZING EFFECT

Over the years, some teachers at Concord High School have become interested in teaching English 11 as a result of catching the spirit of infectious enthusiasm among their colleagues. One teacher who began teaching the course in the 2002–03 school year put it this way: "This course is the best antidote for midcareer burnout. I love teaching this course because I never know how students will respond to the texts. Their responses are so unpredictable and original and fascinating. I feel like I learn about my students more when I'm teaching this course—I really get to know them. I learn myself from seeing their reactions to these ideas."

The energizing effect works as teachers and students come to learn more about each other in ways that contribute to mutual respect. According to Beth York, "There's a connection with these topics that sometimes doesn't happen when we're talking about so much literature that students are unfamiliar with." She described how the course has opened a lot of doorways for her in enhancing the quality of relationships she has been able to build with students. "I've always been very traditional. I never had kids bring in an article, saying, 'Look what I found, Ms. York,' and that kind of thing." But in English 11 her students routinely bring in newspaper articles and talk to her about programs they viewed on television. They insist upon showing her certain websites that she simply must see. Students now let her into their lives outside the classroom, and that provides York with opportunities to understand what knowledge and skills they need. The power of those connections—where students connect what they're experiencing in their life to what's happening in the classroom—is undeniably one of the most compelling features of media literacy education.

One Concord High School teacher who does not teach English 11 told me that "all of the little dinosaurs" who are teaching traditional literature will be dying out in comparison to those who are teaching English 11, since those teachers seem to stay forever young at heart. "You know," said Tareah Gray, "We talk a lot about English 11 at lunch. And the other teachers who aren't teaching it really seem to be interested in what we're doing." She wonders if the other English teachers feel jealous or angry, but she senses that they're just curious. Most of the teachers who are currently teaching English 11 seem to want to keep teaching it the following year. "They just want to keep making it better," she explains. That's comforting for a young teacher, she admits: "You don't acquire these skills overnight. It doesn't all happen magically."

PART II

TEACHING MEDIA LITERACY

Chapter 3

Storytelling Structures, Close Reading, and Point of View

Joanne McGlynn had high hopes for the underachievers as she started teaching English 11 in the fall of 1998. She described one young man, whom we'll call Matthew, who had failed the course twice and was now attending for the third time. "It's a triumph that he has come back—he's coming to a first-period class," she explains, wondering aloud if this new approach to teaching English language arts might just jumpstart Matthew's motivation and engagement to complete high school. A school guidance counselor told her about yet another young man who had come to her and volunteered that this new English 11 course was something he really was going to like. Could this class reach these boys who might not graduate from high school? Would this class be enough to keep them in school? She thought that her focus on the breaking news scandal involving President Clinton might keep their eyes open—after all, it featured sex and lying, two topics of perpetual interest to adolescents. She knew from previous experience that students could discover the power of language—and their own power as communicators—by looking at how the news media shapes our conceptualizations of reality.

English 11 teacher Christine Oskar-Poisson was never going to approach the topic of news and journalism the way that her colleague McGlynn did. Oskar-Poisson valued news and journalism and had a lot of ideas planned for her course. But she was also intrigued with the ways that stories were shaped by storytellers. She wanted to convey the excitement of seeing how a story worked—how it is put together by an author and how different media forms call upon and make possible different approaches to storytelling. She wanted them to understand the concept of point of view deeply, reflecting on the question "Who is telling the story?" in examining the power that storytellers have in society.

This chapter explores the ways English 11 teachers at Concord High School strengthened students' media literacy skills, their information literacy skills, and their understanding of how storytelling works in news, nonfiction, and fiction. Throughout Part II of this book, I describe the curriculum that teachers used to organize the scope of instruction for the Grade 11 Media/Communication course. Examples of student activities, writing, and discussion rely on evidence gathered from interviews with teachers and students, as well as my own observation of classroom sessions. Teachers wove traditional literary analysis activities together with the study of media genres to generate sophisticated opportunities for critical reading and writing activities including essays, fictional stories, historical analysis, screenwriting, and media production. Built within the structure of units which ranged from 2 to 6 weeks of class time, teachers at Concord High School used a combination of viewing, reading, discussion, and writing activities. Student media production, when it did occur, was generally completed outside of class time. None of the teachers did exactly the same kinds of lessons or activities, and only occasionally did teachers share resources like newspaper articles, readings from magazines, or materials found on the Internet.

Concord teachers held the belief that reading, responding to and analyzing texts, and writing were part of a unified cycle of inquiry, problem-solving, and discovery. Teachers routinely used a combination of reading, viewing, seminar-style discussions, and frequent informal writing was a major component of instruction. Much informal writing was done in the context of in-class discussions; these discussions often served as a pre-writing activity that helped students to organize and plan their ideas for more formal writing assignments, where teachers specifically varied the audience, purpose, context, format, and writer's assumed role over the course of the school year. Concord teachers used a large number of short writing assignments that challenged students without overwhelming them, and larger projects were carefully structured to ensure student success. In responding to student writing, teachers typically identified a focus correction area, focusing on one kind of mechanical error and encouraging students to assess their own and peer writing using explicit criteria. All these practices have been articulated by scholars and practitioners who espouse a process approach to the development of students' writing skills (National Writing Project & Nagin, 2003).

In designing the course objectives for English 11, Concord teachers discovered that many of the educational objectives they wanted to emphasize were included on curriculum documents created by state educational leaders for the high school English curriculum. A list of objectives created by English 11 teacher Denise Pariseau reflects the focus of her English 11 course:

• Comprehend, summarize, analyze, and evaluate what you read
• Examine the structure of persuasive arguments
• Interpret and evaluate the use of language and images in literary works
• Examine the effects of word choice, tone, bias, point of view, and structure

- Compose well-organized, persuasive essays
- Incorporate research and critical analysis of topics
- Document a variety of sources
- Recognize emotional appeals, propaganda, and speaker bias
- Recognize structure as part of the message
- Evaluate the competence and credibility of speakers
- Adjust your spoken and written language based on your audience
- Deliver a prepared presentation
- Investigate the source of a media presentation or production—who made it and why
- Understand and evaluate how structure, images, and language influence an audience's emotions and thinking
- Evaluate authenticity, credibility, and context of sources

Each teacher created his or her own list of priorities but teachers often selected outcomes from among the list of objectives articulated in state education frameworks. Some Concord teachers had an expectation that state education leaders would embrace the idea of expanding the concept of text to include audiovisual, mass media, and popular culture materials, as states including Massachusetts, Texas, and North Carolina had done. Texas, for example, has expanded its language arts standards to include "viewing and representing," developed curriculum materials to help teachers integrate media literacy into English, and even showed how these skills link to AP English (Sanders & Tumy, 2006). Sadly, current New Hampshire curriculum documents in English language arts show no evidence of media literacy as an explicit component of the state education frameworks. For example, in describing the reading content knowledge and skills expected of all students, informational texts are defined to include reports, biographies, textbooks, and magazines, but not television programs. Literary texts include novels, epics, plays and poetry, but not film (New Hampshire Department of Education, 2006). In interviewing Concord teachers, I found myself wondering whether Concord teachers were fully aware of what a pioneering enterprise they had embarked upon.

MASTERING THE KEY CONCEPTS OF MEDIA LITERACY

When Joanne McGlynn started in the fall semester of 1998 analyzing the breaking news of the Clinton sex scandal, students' responses weren't what she expected. She showed an episode of the CNN show, *Burden of Proof,* which included an overview of the cast of characters, including Kenneth Starr, the prosecutor; Betty Currie, the president's secretary; and Mike McCurrie, the White House press secretary. Greta Van Susteren began the show by stating:

"Explosive accusations are flying around Washington today. The president is reportedly outraged, reports allege Clinton had a year and a half affair with a White House intern." Then video images showed, in quick succession, a series of denials made by President Clinton:

> The allegations are false and I would never. . .
> I did not have sexual relations with that woman.
> I will await a recommendation from the White House counsel about the institutional responsibilities of the presidency, and when I get it, then I will make a decision.
> This investigation is going on, and you know what the rules for it are. And I just think, as long as it is going on, I should not comment.
> I have nothing else to say.
> I'm looking forward to the opportunity of testifying. I will do so completely and truthfully. I am anxious to do it.

After the class had viewed the attention-getting introduction to the show, McGlynn handed out a list of the five core concepts of media literacy, as shown on Figure 3.1. She had first encountered these ideas during the summer institute she attended at Clark University and hoped that students would internalize these concepts during the course of the school year. By discussing the video examples that she had taped off the air, she intended to illustrate the first three concepts of media literacy: (1) all media messages are constructed; (2) media use symbol systems with codes and conventions to shape messages; and (3) media messages have embedded values and points of view. After viewing and discussing the clip, students were able to explain that the introduction to CNN's *Burden of Proof* was a highly constructed piece that used the powerful technique of video montage editing to show that Clinton was a liar. "So the video montage conveys a point of view all by itself, which makes it seem like the point of view of the hosts of the show are correct and natural," one student summarized. "Just watching on the couch at home, not everyone would recognize how that point of view got shaped by the images they chose for the opening."

The key concepts of media literacy, which were a powerful organizing device for teachers at Concord High School, emerged in the United States in the early 1990s as media literacy scholars and educators synthesized the emerging theoretical literature from literary theory, cultural studies, and media studies (Aufderheide & Firestone, 1993). The work of Cary Bazalgette of the British Film Institute was instrumental in the development of these concepts. In the late 1980s she created a list of "Signpost Questions" that identified focus questions attached to the concepts of agency, genre, technologies, languages, audiences, and representation. Teachers could use these questions in analyzing

Figure 3.1. Five Core Concepts of Media Literacy.

---

1. All media messages are constructed.

2. Media use symbol systems with codes and conventions to shape messages.

3. Media messages have embedded values and points of view.

4. Different people interpret the same media message differently.

5. Most media messages are constructed to gain profit and/or power.

Note. From Thoman and Jolls (2005).

media texts. These "key aspects" stood as clusters of concepts linked to ideas from film study, semiotics, media studies, and cultural studies. Bazalgette (1992) intended these concepts not to constitute a list of knowledge or specific content that should be delivered to students, but "an initial way of organizing one's thinking about the media" (p. 201). In cautioning teachers against using them as a ready-made curriculum, Bazalgette pointed out that these questions were not intended to represent a fixed and permanent framework, but instead they were a way of "provisionally grouping useful concepts in order to link pupils' existing understanding with the learning objectives of a media education curriculum" (p. 204). By the early 1990s, media literacy advocates in the United States had begun introducing these concepts to teachers and found that they were effective in helping K–12 educators develop deeper levels of understanding of the process of analyzing media texts (Hobbs, 1998). Some Concord teachers found it valuable to introduce these concepts explicitly as part of classroom instruction.

In the next period, McGlynn showed students a segment from CNN's *Time Newsstand* (1998), a 7-minute clip that wove together images of President Clinton testifying about his sexual relationship with Monica Lewinsky with images about the decision of the U.S. government to use cruise missiles in Sudan. The United States had just bombed a "terrorist university" and a pharmaceutical plant in Sudan, both linked to Osama bin Laden, the Saudi-born terrorist who had claimed responsibility for the recent bombings of two U.S. embassies in Africa. Using the critical questions, McGlynn said, "We talked about how media messages have their own unique languages." They discussed how the qualities of the video montage combined with the language used by the anchors made it seem like President Clinton was bombing Sudan just to distract the public from his domestic problems.

But students also pointed out how the language of the piece—including key phrases of the voice-over—emphasized the sense of responsibility and focus of the president in taking meaningful action to limit the spread of global terrorism. Others talked about how the fast-paced video montage was sure to attract a large audience of viewers. After discussion, they agreed with the media literacy concepts that (4) different people may interpret the same media message differently and (5) most media messages are constructed to gain profit and/or power. In wrapping up her introduction of the key concepts, McGlynn emphasized that all five concepts are essential to analyzing a text. During the classroom discussion, her attention was heightened by the dynamism of student interaction and the quality of the arguments and ideas that students shared. Afterwards she reflected on the importance of listening carefully and responding thoughtfully to the ideas of her students. English 11 wasn't a classroom where Joanne McGlynn did most of the talking.

In the first weeks of class, she was getting the kind of rich dialogue and active engagement that she wanted from her students. "Normally, it takes them a long while to 'warm up' to talk freely and to share their ideas, but in this class they got right into it. We were having the kind of discussion in September that usually didn't begin until after Christmas," she said. Because students were exploring controversial and current ideas, they knew there were no "right" answers, which may have increased their feelings of competence in participating in a discussion. McGlynn was pleased to see that students valued and respected each others' interpretations yet were also able to interrogate their peers in ways that stretched them. She recognized that those who could articulate their interpretations were helping actively construct an authentic learning experience for themselves and others. As Masterman (1985) has explained, media literacy learning can be nurtured through dialogue, where students can make their own judgments and develop the ability to reflect upon and analyze those judgments. In this context, "The teacher's task is to help everyone concerned make problematic what they think they know and to develop the ability to question underlying assumptions" (p. 28).

THE POWER OF GENRE

In Joanne McGlynn's next class, students engaged in more close reading of a media text. They viewed the same CNN's *Time Newsstand* clip a second time. McGlynn used multiple screenings of a short video in order to strengthen students' analytic skills and promote critical thinking in responding to the text. Just as English teachers use close reading to show students how to read and savor a poem by reading it several times to understand how it makes us feel, how it is constructed, and what devices the poet uses to evoke specific images or feelings, McGlynn applied the same analytic technique to examine segments of television news.

McGlynn recalled that one student noticed that images of President Clinton were briefly intercut with an image of Hillary Rodham Clinton, who was looking distraught. As McGlynn invited a student to use the pause button on the remote control to freeze the tape, one student said, "Those pictures of Hillary, they look like file photos." The student, whose father is a TV producer, then explained what she had learned from her dad about file photos. She launched into an informal definition, explaining different genres of photojournalism and making distinctions among a *file photo*, a *news photo*, and a *portrait*. The first time a photograph is used, it will normally be in the genre for which it is produced. For example, a *news photo*—an image of an event—will be placed on a website or in a newspaper. A *portrait* will be used in connection with an interview. But after a photograph has been used once, it becomes part of the archives; it becomes a *file photo* with its own potentially long life. Once in the archives, a file photo can be edited so that an image, originally used as a news photo, can become a picture that is used and understood by the audience as a portrait.

Staring at the still image paused on the screen, McGlynn asked the class, "When do you think that picture was taken?" Students responded that it may have been taken 2 years ago. They then reflected on the fact that the segment looked archival because it was presented in tones of black and white, not color. "So the decision to make the footage in black and white is a way that the TV producers are using the language of TV news to communicate," said one student a little tentatively, with a sense of discovery in his voice. McGlynn added, "And the different types of photos—news photos, file photos, and portraits—are examples of the codes and conventions that are associated with images we see in the news." Using familiar nonliterary forms of communication and expression (like photographs and TV shows) helps students more deeply consider the concept of *genre* and its role in the meaning-making process.

Genres are those classifications given to texts that position the text in relation to other similar works. In literature, categories like poetry, drama, comedy, biography, satire, novel, tragedy, or short story are common genres. In film, categories like documentary, animation, romance, action-adventure, and science fiction are just a few of many examples. Texts can be classified using multiple genres, and new genres emerge and transform over time. According to communication scholars and literary critics, all texts exist within a genre (Chandler, 2002). But genres are more than just devices to classify texts; they shape readers' expectations and thus influence the meaning-making process. For example, when I read the newspaper, I expect the photographs to be informative; when I go to the art gallery, I expect the photographs I see there to be artistic. When I go to the bookstore and pick up a biography, I expect it to tell me about the life and times of an individual, but when I pick up a memoir, I know that it will be a more personal and intimate reflection of the author's own life experiences. Moreover, my expectations for a genre might be different from others', because my understanding of a particular genre has been generated by my own prior experiences with different types of texts. Genres operate to position the relationship between the reader and the text:

> Every genre positions those who participate in a text of that kind: as interviewer or interviewee, as listener or storyteller, as a reader or a writer, as a person interested in political matters, as someone to be instructed or as someone who instructs; each of these positionings implies different possibilities for response and for action. Each written text provides a "reading position" for readers, a position constructed by the writer for the "ideal reader" of the text. (Kress, 1988, p. 107)

That day in class, McGlynn didn't expect that the concept of genre would be introduced—she was focused on introducing those key concepts of media literacy. But in seeing the learning experience materialize before her eyes through the contributions of students in sharing ideas, she appreciated how, by using the power of dialogue, an authentic learning experience had emerged that would help shape the unique character of her English 11 class.

OBJECTIVITY, BIAS, AND BALANCE: WHAT'S NEWSWORTHY?

When exploring the point of view presented in the CNN *Time Newsstand* segment, Joanne McGlynn asked her students to describe the point of view depicted in the segment. Her students mostly agreed that the story presented President Clinton in a positive light overall. One student said, "He screwed up in what he did, but this piece shows that even though he screwed up, he was making really serious decisions." They wanted to continue talking about whether Clinton's actions were ethical, and McGlynn steered them away, saying, "Truly, that's not my interest in this course. In this course, what I want to know is what CNN did in the way they put the segment together—was that ethical?"

One student replied, "You know, maybe they shouldn't be telling us that Clinton is a good guy or a bad guy. But you know what? The piece we watched on CNN the other day [CNN's *Burden of Proof*] showed Clinton in a negative light. And now this piece is more positive. Maybe CNN is giving us a little balance."

Good point, she thought at the time. But although balance is important, truth is even more important. The student's conceptualization of balance enabled McGlynn to engage her students on the stated purpose of journalism: the practical and functional search for truth. More than the mantra of accuracy, fairness, and balance, Kovach and Rosenstiel (2001) explain that, from a journalistic point of view, truth can be seen as a goal, a process over time. Calling journalism a discipline of verification, they write, "Balancing a story by being fair to both sides may not be fair to the truth. Seen in this light, fairness and balance take on a new meaning. Rather than high principles, they are really techniques—devices—to help guide journalists in the development and verification of their accounts" (p. 77).

Most high school students are not active news consumers. According to statistics, only 28% of teens look at a daily newspaper (Gallup Youth Poll, 2004). English 11 teachers recognized that, for most students, the news/journalism unit would be their first extensive experience with informational texts in the context of an English language arts class. Heather Ouellette-Cygan spent considerable time using the Concord *Monitor* as a text in her class. Mike Robb Grieco also wanted to give his students some hands-on experience exploring the contents of a newspaper. He introduced them to the role of journalism in society by first asking students to create a unique, personal version of a newspaper. In an assignment he called "News to Me," students were asked to cut and paste newspapers to create a personal news sheet reflecting their own vision of what is (and is not) newsworthy. On the first page of their four-page spread, students were to locate, select, and arrange articles that represented information they like to read about and think is important to know. On the second page, students placed content that people should know about because of its importance. On the third page, students placed content that they personally did not care about but still thought was newsworthy. On the final page, students placed content that was not newsworthy and did not appeal to them. Then students wrote a reflective essay about their choices. According to Robb Grieco, "The physical activity of reading and making choices enabled students to create a personal connection to the news, recognizing the elements of storytelling at work in both the informational and entertainment elements of a newspaper." Aware of the importance of creating among students a sense of personal connection to the topic, English 11 teachers found ways to invite students to consider and reflect upon current events as they are presented daily in the newspaper and on TV news.

English 11 students learned that, as gatekeepers, news media professionals decide what information to select and what to omit. Gatekeepers control the public's knowledge of events through this process of selection, emphasis, and omission. Media gatekeeping is based on principles of *news values*, the routine criteria used by journalists to decide what is newsworthy. A person, event, or occurrence may be considered newsworthy if it features people designated as those with high status, if it's considered relevant to the target audience, if it includes controversy or conflict, or if it has human interest appeal. Dramatic, unpredictable, or novel events and information are often considered newsworthy (Fuller, 1996; Schudson, 1995).

A number of English 11 teachers presented a list of criteria for determining whether an event is newsworthy; others presented various definitions of newsworthiness in order to encourage students to understand the logic operating in the newsroom. Students had different perspectives and emotional responses when they learned about how journalistic decision making affects the content of the news. One student in McGlynn's class said, "The media try to control you in a certain way. They choose to show you certain things that they want you to know about. They emphasize what they think is important." Another said, "Now when I watch the news, I think about it and how it's structured. It kind of makes me mad sometimes. You can't watch it without thinking." Another talked about how she looks at media differently, explaining that before taking this class, she would "watch TV or look through a newspaper and it would just be a newspaper" and she would take the information and entertainment at face value. Now, she explained, "You see in-depth, a whole bunch of other stuff that you didn't see before." For example, explained another student, this course has shown "how it's all connected. Disney owns a bunch of radio stations and ABC." This student pointed out that he now recognizes how a corporation communicates their opinions using many different types of communications media. Before taking this class, "You never knew that you were still being fed Disney products."

MEDIA OWNERSHIP

Many English 11 teachers addressed the topic of media ownership. When an issue of *Brill's Content* magazine featured an attention-getting cover with a cross-sectional drawing of a human brain, the teachers were thrilled. The cover showed an image of the various biological structures of the cerebrum, cortex, cerebellum, and the brain stem renamed as News Corporation, Viacom/CBS, Time Warner, Disney, and AT&T. English 11 teachers used an article from the magazine entitled "Why Media Mergers Matter" (Rosenwein, 2000). It was a challenging piece for high schoolers that introduced them to the various perceptions among media professionals about the increased centralization of ownership of media industries. Words from the article, like *synergy, oligarchy, aversion,* and *myriad* served to support students' vocabulary study. A pullout map depicting the tangled network of joint ventures and economic relationships between big media companies helped students begin to identify how cable networks and record companies were part of much larger firms. Short essays from writers, producers, and editors including David Denby, Harry Shearer, Scott Turow, and David Crane were used to help students map the diverse complex perspectives on this topic. After their reading, some English 11 teachers asked students to generate a list of the advantages and disadvantages of increased centralization of media ownership, reflecting the different points of view presented in the reading, including perspectives from consumers, creative media professionals, and managers of media companies. This practice supported students reading comprehension skills while inviting them to reflect on their own stance in relation to the ideas. To discover how concentrated an average person's media diet has become in the age of Big Media, the magazine reported on 10 people's media use habits for a single day and created mini-mind-maps showing how much influence the major conglomerates had upon each individual. English 11 students re-created the report for themselves, keeping a media diary for a day and then finding out which companies owned the books, TV shows, music, and videogames they had used that day and drawing a picture of Big Media's influence on their minds. After these activities, students wrote more formal five-paragraph essays on the topic, developing a thesis statement and using reasoning and evidence to support their ideas.

In 2003, when the FCC considered relaxing media ownership rules, students followed the story in the news, finding only very limited coverage of the event. As Robert McChesney (2004) has explained, "Despite all the activity and despite evidence that the American people were concerned about the issue, the media reform movement was almost entirely outside the mainstream political culture and invisible within commercial news media" (p. 255). So when the National Conference on Media Reform met in Madison, Wisconsin, in 2003, some English 11 teachers talked about the conference with students and invited students to learn more about the coalition of activist groups participating in the event. Students reviewed the websites of various organizations, including Move On, Media Transparency, Z Magazine, Fairness and Accuracy in Reporting, and the Free Speech Network. In helping students move from consumer to citizen, it was important for them to learn about the alternative information sources that people can use to translate ideas into action.

HOW IMAGES WORK AS TEXTS

Most English 11 teachers were less comfortable in the arena of exploring the political and economic issues concerning media industries and more comfortable in including a substantial focus on the ways that images work as texts. Val Aubry regularly asked students to "read" news photos and offer up written interpretations that included analysis of the compositional elements of the image. For example, students were asked to use the Internet to select a photo from a news media source. Students wrote structured essays where they described the picture's content, analyzed the author's motivations by considering the implicit and explicit purposes, and identified the emotional tone of the photo using descriptive writing and inference making. Many lively discussions ensued as students discussed the iconic images that were presented by the U.S. media during the invasion of Iraq in 2003 as part of the government's public relations campaign, including images that showed the toppling of the statue of Saddam Hussein. One student wrote about a news photo that depicted fresh faces of young Iraqis holding up images of George Bush, which had the words *hero* and *friend* written on them in English and Arabic. He wrote, "A reader would feel that the people are happy and satisfied at the latest developments of the war. The young boy in the front of the picture is wearing a shirt that is brighter than the people behind him. This makes him stand out even more, accompanied by the great smile on his face." The student continued, "In the picture, it seems like there is a massive crowd but that might not be the case. It might in fact be less than 10 people that are in jubilation but, by just looking at it, you might think it is an entire nation."

Joanne McGlynn asked students to read and discuss "The Power of Images" (Davis, 1992), a short essay available from the Center for Media Literacy. Exploring how the overwhelming flow of images in contemporary culture carry with them a set of values and ideologies, the author lists six myths that are embedded in the images we see on television and in newspapers and magazines. These include "Your body is not good enough" and "The world is a dangerous place, and we need guns, police, and military to protect us." McGlynn liked the way the article traced the historical shifts from oral to written to image-based culture. It was early in the semester, and in discussing this article, one young man stated, "Well, the one good thing about photographs is that at least they're objective." Clearly, McGlynn thought to herself as she considered how to respond, he hadn't really comprehended the article. So she pulled out her magazine file on the spot and showed students the *Time* and *Newsweek* magazine covers from June 27, 1994, the pair of photos showing O. J. Simpson's face electronically altered for the *Newsweek* cover. "Whatever you can say about photos, you can't call them objective," McGlynn explained. Students enjoyed sharing their knowledge of how digital techniques made it possible to manipulate photos. McGlynn was pleasantly surprised to see Matthew, her underachiever, explain to the class in great detail that photographs were no longer objective and that, if you wanted to, you could make a very realistic photograph showing a flying saucer attacking the city of Concord.

LOOKING AT LITERATURE: IT'S ALL IN YOUR POINT OF VIEW

Val Aubry recognized how the concept of point of view could be developed within the course and was delighted to be able to introduce her students to William Faulkner's *As I Lay Dying* (1930/1957) as part of English 11. While many English teachers include a Faulkner short story or his famous Nobel Prize speech, the use of one of his major novels, *As I Lay Dying*, is not common in high schools. Aubry liked to use it for the opportunity to explore how characters are created by authors and how character motivations shape the narrative. The novel is told in stream-of-consciousness fashion by 15 different speakers in some 59 chapters. In its depiction of the Bundren family's quest to bury their dead matriarch, Addie, in her own hometown, against the threats of flood and fire, the novel explores the nature of grieving, community, and family. As one student explained, "*As I Lay Dying* has different points of view. Every chapter was the voice of a different character." After reading the novel, Aubry asked the students to create a family tree of the Bundren family and to create a book cover for the book using a powerful visual image that conveyed some aspect of the story to readers.

She also made a creative writing assignment in which students had to write a story showing the distinctive point of view of at least three characters. One student reported, "I thought it would be easy to write different points of view—but it was actually kind of hard to make the story understandable with all those voices. And it's hard to imagine other points of view—if you're only one person, you have your view. But in writing, you have to pretend you're someone else." Aubry commented on how much she appreciated student writing because, through it, she can see them working on ideas. She explained, "They are thinking and formulating thought. And they're organizing what they're going to say."

During their reading of *As I Lay Dying*, Aubry invited students to examine how the language choices a character makes shapes the way readers perceive them. She asked students to select key passages, short excerpts that illustrate some aspect of the character, plot, or point of view of the author. "These key passages keep kids anchored to the source—they don't just talk off the top of your head. They use evidence to support their ideas," explained Aubry.

Students' language abilities are a function of their thinking, and teachers at Concord High School wanted to encourage their enjoyment of literature and help them develop proficiency in writing, reading, speaking, listening, viewing, and representing. Val Aubry and all the Concord High School teachers wanted to promote students' personal growth and social development through expanding their knowledge and use of language and their understanding of the human condition. So when it came to vocabulary study, Aubry was not the kind of teacher who spent large amounts of time on test prep. Like many teachers, she had already observed that her most able students were adept at defining such terms as *allegory* and *dactyl*. As one author explains,

> [Students] found it difficult to summarize an essayist's argument or to para-phrase a poem. These skills demanded approaching works as wholes, as readers had always approached them. But these students, raised on aptitude tests, were less readers of books than scanners of texts. They searched not for the "soul" of a work but for the indispensable bit of information. While they had little passion for reading, they read more for coursework than ever before—they had to on account of increased academic requirements and heightened competition for admission to top colleges. But most found the notion that a book could change a life incomprehensible. "How could that be?" they wondered when I told them that [a book] had once altered the way people saw the world. Reading, like taking a test, was becoming a utilitarian task; it was useful for careers, but not for life. (Ruenzel, 2004, p. 247)

With all the emphasis on SAT scores and getting into elite colleges, many teachers recognize that their best students may approach high school English class like just another hoop to jump through on the way to graduation. Aubry wanted to be able to explore literary works and develop students' reading and writing skills to give them an increased sense of personal agency and help them appreciate the broader issues related to the functions of storytelling in a sociocultural context.

Storytellers compose using print and nonprint media to shape our sense of ourselves, our world, the nature of the human experience, and our own possibilities as human beings. It's among the most powerful of roles in society. According to Aubry, media literacy helped her get this message to a wider range of students, those who might be very bright but were just "going through the motions" as well as those with less natural ability who had long ago decided that they weren't "into" English class. "The kids who normally tune out of English, they're getting really pulled into this thing," she explained when I interviewed her in the middle of the 1998–99 school year. She described the case of one student, a young man who flunked the first quarter because he didn't want to have to do the reading. "Now, all of a sudden, he's producing top-notch stuff."

When it came time for the English 11 midterm examination on the journalism unit, Aubry's students knew it wouldn't be a multiple choice test; it would be a series of questions that students would address in one-paragraph to one-page answers. Students were required to stay in the room for 90 minutes, but they could take up to 2 ½ hours to complete the exam. Questions included items like: "Explain Pete Hamill's concept of *zocalo* as it applies to newspapers" and "Recently a *New York Times* reporter, Jayson Blair, resigned in the midst of a scandal. Explain what had happened to cause his resignation and why the newspaper was so upset about the situation." The exam included reproductions of two news photographs and asked students to describe each shot in detail and explain why it was chosen for publication, including information about composition, subject matter, perspective, and intended audience. She remembers being astounded when two thirds of the class remained in their seats as the exam ended. "I never had kids that devoted to anything. They left the room saying, 'I didn't say enough about this.' I've never had so many kids be this enthusiastic about English class."

MEDIA COMPOSITION: AN APPROACH TO ADAPTATION

As a veteran language arts educator with a Ph.D. in education, Val Aubry had long recognized the power of creative writing to develop students' literacy skills. She created an assignment that involved students in an intense collaborative media production project that required imagination, planning, and creativity. The assignment: Plan a television program that will relate the story of *As I Lay Dying* in one 30-minute time slot on network television. Working together in teams of three, students were required to produce an overview that described their TV show concept, and they also needed to provide a rationale for their approach. Then each group member was responsible for producing one of the following: (1) a storyboard depicting the sequence of scenes in the program, (2) a transcript of an interview with at least one of the participants in the program, and (3) a screenplay or detailed description of one 3- to 5-minute scene. Student teams either made an oral presentation describing their program or created a video depicting their program concept. Students worked both inside and outside of class to prepare their presentations or videos. Figure 3.2 shows an excerpt from the assignment. Aubry had designed an ambitious assignment that tapped students' ability to compose ideas and express themselves through adaprtation.

Students showed creativity in approaching this task. Many students used their home video equipment to create short scenes of the television program concept they had imagined. One team of students used the genre of the thriller to present this story, portraying the character of Vardaman as jealous and deranged, verging on evil. They made much visual drama of the scene where he drills holes in his mother's casket "so she can breathe," and they played up the "blood and gore" in the scene where, after catching a big fish, he cleaned it by hacking it up with an ax. In writing to explain his group's rationale for the group's choice of genre, one student wrote: "Thrillers and horror films are popular now and have been equally popular in the past. People for some odd reason find it very appealing to feel the fear of the characters."

Another team of students adapted the plot of *As I Lay Dying* as a court-room-based drama. In writing a scene for the show, they created the character of a prosecuting attorney who struts before the judge and explains, "I would like to bring before the court the story of a woman that took care of and watched over her family, and what did they give her in return? Thirty years of pain and sorrow, and all she wanted to do was die."

Another group told the story using a newsmagazine format with Darl and Jewel Bundren as the main characters in an episode of *20/20,* along with Barbara Walters as the interviewer, who is represented in the students' video as a cardboard cutout seated along with members of the Bundren family in a comfortable living room set. In the video, Darl's confession was part of the TV interview: Responding to a question, he explains why he burned down the barn and how embarrassed he was by the stench of his mother's decomposing body on the long trip.

Still another team situated the Bundren family on the courtroom reality TV show *Judge Judy,* where viewers learn that Anse Bundren, who had gotten everything he wanted at the end of the novel, has completely disregarded the memory of his badly treated wife. In their episode, she is alive and is pursuing legal action against her husband, seeking a divorce. A student explained the group's rationale, writing, "We wanted to do something that focused on Addie because we felt that she didn't get much of a chance to speak her opinion in the book. We fashioned the family's behavior in court around their dys-functional tendencies and concluded the case with Addie's victory because we felt it was justice."

In England, researchers have found that the most effective multimedia productions by young people incorporated genres and forms that were familiar to them, like the horror genre (Buckingham, 2003b; Hart & Hicks, 2002). The process of digital media production allows for the internalization of abstract concepts of genre, narrative, and audience. Burn and Leach (2004) write, "Cultural experience and the media discourses . . . provide the semiotic raw material for their work, as well as modeling the kinds of structures they build in their own video, multimedia or writing" (p. 164). Getting the chance to write scripts, draw storyboards, and compose short videos based on literature was not only pleasurable and motivating, it also helped students appreciate storytelling techniques used in film and media. It built their ability to recognize structural devices in narrative. It strengthened their ability to communicate effectively in a small team and to work through the steps in a complex process. One student explained, "If you're making a movie, you can't just have a stationary camera sitting there, filming a whole movie from that position. You've got to move around."

Through this assignment, William Faulkner's novel had come alive, quite literally, in the imaginations of those English 11 students who tried their hand at the challenge of adaptation. Using brainstorming, planning, writing, drawing, and the lenses of their home video equipment, they worked in teams to retell a story using images, language, and sound. In teaching writing and composition, much of the creative process can be understood as an intertextual process (Alvermann, 1999). In learning to write, "what the student needs from the teacher is help in seeing discourse structures themselves in all their fullness and their power" (Scholes, 1985, p. 144). When students recognized how Faulkner manipulated readers' perceptions through his strategic use of point of view, they were then able to play with rhetorical devices as storytellers themselves.

INFORMATION LITERACY IN ENGLISH LANGUAGE ARTS

Most English teachers love fiction and are less comfortable using expository texts in the classroom. Some teachers hold the belief that informational texts are less creative and inspiring to young readers, and historically, studies have shown that students prefer narrative to informational material (Sebesta & Monson, 2003). But the rise of the Internet, as the fastest growing communication tool ever, has led to an increased appreciation for the value of source evaluation as a component of formal instruction in English language arts (Kinzer & Leander, 2003). *Information literacy* has been defined as a set of abilities requiring individuals to recognize when information is needed and have the ability to locate, evaluate, and use it (American Library Association & American Association of School Librarians, 1991). At the heart of it, information literacy emphasizes the need for careful selection, retrieval, evaluation, and choice making in response to the abundant information available in the workplace, at school, and in all aspects of personal decision making, especially in the areas of citizenship and health (Plotnick, 1999).

Information literacy education emphasizes the analytic, metacognitive, and procedural knowledge needed to use information in specific domains, fields, and contexts. A primary emphasis is placed on recognizing message quality, authenticity, and source credibility. School library media specialists have discovered that personal and contextual factors activate or suppress young people's evaluative stance toward information, finding that under some conditions they are likely to critically assess information or accept information at face value (Fitzgerald, 1999). Since the process of finding, using, and handling information is always context-specific, it is never only just a routine application of cookbook-like instructions. In line with this perspective, some teachers see information literacy more broadly and more closely akin to processes involved in reading.

High school English teachers at Concord High were responsible for

Figure 3.2. *As I Lay Dying:* A Docudrama Project.

One media development in the 1980s was the *docudrama*, a program that portrays a real-life situation in fictional form. While they are based on real situations, these shows tended to take liberties with the facts in order to heighten the dramatic effect of the events depicted. The may also choose to tell the story from the viewpoints that are most likely to elicit emotions (and ratings).

Although William Faulkner's *As I Lay Dying* is fictional to begin with, the multiple characters all tell the story from their own viewpoints. As a result, the book tends to leave the reader in much the same situation as does a docudrama—wondering just what was factual and how each character shapes their story and conceals their motivations in order to elicit the most empathy.

Your job is to plan a television program that will relate the story of *As I Lay Dying.* You will have one 30-minute slot on network TV to tell how the Bundren family took their mother's body to Jefferson. You should work in teams of three to accomplish the task. Your final product will be judged based on the understanding it reflects both of the novel itself and of the process of creating a media message.

There are five components to the project. Two of these involve considerable planning and should be completed by the group working together:

1. An overview of the program that will describe your approach to the story, outline the sequence of scenes you will dramatize, and delineate the characters and narrators if any) who will be program's focus
2. A brief rationale for your particular approach

The other three components should be completed separately (one by each member of the group), based on the group decisions:

3. A storyboard depicting the sequence of scenes in the program.
4. A transcript of an interview with at least one of the participants in the docudrama.
5. A screenplay (or otherwise detailed description) of one 3-to-5 minute scene.

Remember that you are constructing a message that will be viewed by a large number of people—or your ratings will be poor. Think about how you can best dramatize the Bundren family journey to gain empathy for their struggle. Obviously, you cannot tell the whole story. What you will choose to make their journey understandable and appealing to the audience? How will you hook your audience? How will you use media elements to heighten the effectiveness of your program?

Note. Activity developed by Val Aubry.

teaching the students the process of writing a research paper. But like other English teachers in the United States, they had various levels of engagement (or disengagement) with this task. Some teachers intend to have students write a research paper, but place it at a time period in the semester where it gets short shrift or is skipped altogether. Older teachers may not be familiar with contemporary methods of locating and finding information using online databases and still require students to use old-fashioned methods of research (i.e., 3" x 5" note cards). Teachers may or may not actively collaborate with school librarians on the design of assignments. Others delegate instruction on source evaluation to the school librarian. Only a few high school English teachers tackle the challenge of teaching research skills and writing nonfiction reports with enthusiasm and gusto.

Scholars have pointed out that the evaluation of sources has traditionally been seriously underemphasized in language arts education. As a result, students are likely to develop evaluation skills tacitly rather than through school-based curriculum and instruction (Kinzer & Leander, 2003). Lacking opportunities for staff development to help build knowledge and skills, teachers may find themselves in a position of ignoring these issues in the classroom or inventing, borrowing, or modifying lesson plans and activities in a superficial way, often without a fundamental understanding of underlying conceptual issues.

Concord High School English 11 teachers had a shared interest in strengthening students' ability to evaluate the quality of information and ideas, but not all placed equal emphasis on having students write research papers. Val Aubry designed a research paper assignment that involved students in analyzing how different types of news outlets presented particular news stories. At the time of my interview with her in 1999, Aubry described a student who had just chosen to write his paper about the press coverage of Dr. Jack Kevorkian. Kevorkian was on trial for giving a lethal injection to a man suffering from Lou Gehrig's disease, a fatal illness that leaves victims unable to speak, swallow, or move. Film showing the administration of the drug had been shown on the CBS show, *60 Minutes*. For 16- and 17-year-old students, the challenge was to step beyond the highly emotional and ethically complex content of the news story to examine the way messages were shaped. Aubry explained, "The kid originally wanted to write on the content issue—the controversy about doctor-assisted suicide—but I encouraged her to focus on examining the structure and framing of the issues as presented on television and in the newsmagazines. She did an amazing job."

Another student wrote about the 20 skiers in a cable car who plunged 300 feet to their deaths in February 1998 when U.S. pilots, training in Italy, sliced through the cable when they were flying too low and too fast in the Italian Alps. Aubry explained, "He contrasted the way the U.S. press emphasized the event as 'an accident' while newspapers in Germany emphasized the idea of the soldiers 'joy riding.'"The student went on to develop a thoughtful, sophisticated argument about the power of language to shape our conceptualization of reality. In past years, Aubry had found it tedious to read students' research papers (which were often on a very narrow range of topics with a focus on simple factual presentation of information). This approach to teaching the research paper, with its focus on comparing and contrasting news coverage of a single event, generated a much wider range of topics and included clear evidence of students' critical thinking. She recognized students' unique voices in their writing and did not find many examples of cut-and-paste plagiarism. Aubry found them to be a pleasure to read and she enjoyed sharing them among students so they could read each other's work as well.

LIBRARY RESEARCH, CURIOSITY, AND THE MEANINGS OF MOTIVATION

Many students arrive in high school without a real appreciation for the internal joys associated with the search for knowledge. Researchers have found that engaged readers have strategic knowledge about printed texts, use reading to gain knowledge, and are involved in the social dimensions of reading. Learners increase their motivation when they have opportunities for choice, challenge, social interaction, and success (Morrow, 2003). When learners stop coordinating their own personal interests with academic tasks, they lose motivation. They become unable to sustain the attention that these tasks require. By contrast, when literacy becomes a lifestyle, seeking insights and being engaged in the quest for knowledge becomes a matter of following one's intellectual heart (Thorkildsen, 2002). In communities where testing and evaluation are central, educators have no time to cultivate the habits of mind that may support the development of an adolescent's lifelong motivation and engagement.

Most Concord High English 11 faculty found creative ways to develop students' curiosity and interest in gathering information and reporting research by using a library. In order to explore how cultural expectations, personal experiences, and mass marketing concerns affect reporting on news events, teachers assigned one or more research activities. For example, English 11 teachers asked students to select a current events story and find three sources from newspapers, magazines, or electronic or digital media. Then they were asked to either find or conduct an interview with one of the principals involved in the story or interview someone about his or her reaction to the story. Students were asked to analyze the evidence using the five critical questions (introduced in Chapter 1) and record their conclusions in a 4–5 page paper. In Val Aubry's class, one student wrote about the different representations of the victims of the sexual abuse scandal in the Archdiocese of Boston, interviewing her father about his interpretation of the news event. Another student compared British and local news sources on the coverage of antiwar protests, finding that local news sources trivialized protesters. Commenting on the headline of one article from the Concord *Monitor,* he wrote, "This made it seem as if it was a prowar rally where some antiwar folk showed up." The student explained that the newspaper took pains to balance the story to include prowar perspectives because of its diverse readership. When this student interviewed a local peace activist, he learned that press coverage of protest is a key element of social change. By actively constructing original knowledge through conducting an interview, the literacy process becomes more authentic, personal, and intimate. This creates a link between the information constructed by others (the materials students found in the library and online) and students' lived experience as constructors of meaning themselves.

Mike Robb Grieco sought to ignite students' intellectual curiosity and build their confidence through an activity called the I-Search, a project that brings a student-centered learning experience to the processes of library research and literacy development (Zorfass & Copel, 1995). Robb Grieco conceptualized his I-Search as an ambitious daylong field trip to the main library at the University of New Hampshire in Durham. He hoped that a field trip would inspire his students to discover the pleasures of following their own path of independent learning while basking in the vastness of knowledge and ideas available at a university library. He playfully entitled the assignment, "My Day of Intellectual Leisure at the Dimond Library." Students had several short writing assignments to complete during the day and for homework. On the bus ride from Concord to Durham, students were asked to write down their preliminary focus questions, some topics that would be fun to research. At the university library, students worked independently, browsing the stacks and searching for materials from which to learn. Robb Grieco urged, "Allow yourself some freedom to change your focus according to what catches your curiosity most. If you see some books that intrigue you while you browse, indulge yourself." Students were asked to select five books or resource materials to settle down with and spend time with. At two designated times, students were asked to write journal entries summarizing what they had learned and reflecting on their exploration. On the bus ride home, students were asked to share their findings in conversation with five other students, taking notes about what they learned from their peers. At home, they wrote two journal entries describing what they had learned on the bus ride from their peers and reflecting on the overall experience of the day.

One student began his day of intellectual leisure by wandering around the library. In browsing, he was surprised to find a whole shelf of books about languages. "Every book had a different topic and some of them were even written in foreign languages," he noted in his first journal entry. Settling down by a sunny window with five books, his second journal entry shared some of what he'd learned. "German is the only language in which all nouns begin with a capital letter." He discovered new questions that interested him: What is the history of spoken language? What was the development of language? What is the difference between dialects? Why isn't there a world language? When was the first written language recorded? He wrote, "Languages are something that I might consider studying if I go to college. This information gave me a greater respect for anyone who can fluently speak a second language." On the bus ride home, he talked with another boy who had learned that animals communicate even though they don't use language. His friend Adam informed him that ALF stands for Alien Life Form. One of the girls had learned about Freud's theory of dreams and the unconscious mind. Another had discovered the *Encyclopedia on Death*, with its sections on "Fear and Anxiety" and "Epitaphs." Still another student looked into the royal family of England, explaining how all royalty were related through intermarriage. In reflecting on the learning experience, he wrote, "The atmosphere made me want to learn and write this essay and that's saying a lot. All in all, I liked the place, and no, it wasn't boring."

A lot of students have discovered a way to survive the often oppressive and controlling environment of schools by camouflaging their intellectual life in order to conform to the expectations of educators and peers. "Knowing things that cannot be shared with others in one's environment can create a sense of isolation," explains Thorkildsen (2002, p. 331) in describing the barriers that educators sometimes set up, unknowingly, when they limit students' ability to feel comfortable in sharing their own unique interests. Schools and classrooms can be structured to support or diminish a student's growth as an independent learner. As the convergence of media and technologies provide so much information and ideas so easily at the touch of the fingertip, the opportunity to give every student a joyful experience in knowledge discovery is easier than ever before. English 11 teachers tried to reinvent the traditional research paper by designing learning experiences that built upon students' existing knowledge, interests, and social relationships, and involved them in exercising their curiosity and cultivating their own stances as active participants in the creation of meaning.

In this chapter, readers have learned how English 11 teachers at Concord High School used reading, viewing, discussion, and writing in a sequence of activities designed to promote inquiry, critical thinking, and communication skills. Students in English 11 shaped the course by the ways they actively engaged with ideas, creating high levels of dynamic involvement and participation that jump-started the learning experience in September and helped sustain it all year. They discovered the power of simple key questions and close reading to interrogate a text for meaning. Students deepened their appreciation of the power of language and images as a means of social control, exploring point of view and bias in the news media and considering how issues of media ownership affect what they see in mainstream media. Teachers helped promote curiosity by inspiring students to think of themselves as independent learners. Working in teams on a video production gave them an appreciation for the complexity of adaptation. They began to see media texts as carefully constructed works of symbolic expression designed to accomplish a particular purpose or goal. And students had repeated opportunities to develop their own voices by composing messages using writing and speech and visual imagery and digital technology, to discover the power of communication for themselves.

Chapter 4

Advertising, Persuasion, and Propaganda

Joanne McGlynn was right in the middle of her 6-week unit on advertising when I arrived for a visit. How did she feel about it so far? "It's exhausting and exhilarating. At first, I didn't know what to do. But then I realized I have a lot of resources, and really, there's too much for just 6 weeks." McGlynn listed some of the resources she had already used in her class: a video from the Canadian video series, *Scanning Television* about cat lovers who protest a car commercial that shows a cat at risk; an excerpt from Neil Postman's book, *Technopoly;* a *New York Times* article about the Superbowl; a critical analysis of a single commercial that she found in the business section of *USA Today.* And of course, like most of her colleagues, she had started the unit with the conventional English language arts activity in which students were given a long list of rhetorical and persuasive techniques (i.e., humor, testimonial, repetition, name calling, hyperbole, plain folks) and asked to find examples of these techniques on television and radio advertising. And she'd finish the unit by having students read *1984* or *Brave New World.* After she outlined the plan in detail, she reflected that it might take 8 weeks.

In incorporating the topic of advertising, propaganda, and persuasion into the English 11 course, McGlynn and her faculty colleagues at Concord High School were trying to integrate a number of concepts into the domain of English language arts: target audience, branding, the rhetorical structure of persuasive appeals, language and power, and the role of consumption and entertainment as cultural values. Teachers used advertising texts to practice discerning the connotative, denotative, and associative meanings of language and images that were explicit or implied. According to Mike Robb Grieco, "This training helped connect with students' understanding of poetic and literary devices in literature." This theme also raised the intriguing and difficult questions for teachers and students about the relationship between people and products in a consumer society.

THE STUDY OF PROPAGANDA:
A LONG TRADITION IN ENGLISH LANGUAGE ARTS

In many classrooms in the United States, Great Britain, Canada, and Australia, advertising is a topic of inquiry, and print and TV ads are used in classrooms as "texts" to be studied. Advertising has been studied in high school since the early 1950s, when post–World War II educators recognized the need to introduce the concepts of propaganda and public opinion. In 1950, books like *Radio, Television and Society* (Siepmann, 1950) explained the role of advertising in the dominant mass medium of the time—radio— helping readers understand that radio's limited format of dramas, soap operas, information broadcasts, and children's programs reflected the advertisers' interest in attracting a mass audience. Although trivialized by academics who dismissed the then-novel genre of pop sociology, Vance Packard's *The Hidden Persuaders* (1957) sold a million copies, revealing the techniques of psychological manipulation used to sell toothpaste, cars, and cigarettes. Some more senior Concord teachers remembered this book, which exposed the marketing secrets used in advertising and offered a stinging indictment of advertisers' attempts to use the tools of psychology to massage and mold our inner thoughts, fears, and dreams for profit. The book had caused a sensation when it appeared, and some English 11 teachers remembered their own youthful discussions about advertising and propaganda. The press of the time captured the spirit of resistance: "We have reached the sad age when minds and not just houses can be broken and entered," concluded *The New Yorker.* Thundered the *Saturday Evening Post*: "The subconscious mind is the most delicate part of the most delicate apparatus in the entire universe. . . . It is not to be smudged, sullied or twisted in order to boost the sales of popcorn or anything else" (Shalit, 1999, p. 1).

By the late 1950s, when Marshall McLuhan's visit to New York City introduced students at Columbia's Teachers College to the relationship among mass media, communication, and education, a number of teachers at the secondary level had begun introducing the study of media and advertising into English language arts. For example, older teachers watched Neil Postman's early morning show on *Sunrise Semester,* a nationally broadcast educational television program. For teachers of this generation, McLuhan and Postman provided the first exposure to how to teach about media, propaganda, and public opinion. By the 1970s, high school English language arts teachers were writing about their efforts to examine the use of language for deceitful purposes, manipulation, and social control (Burmester, 1974). Alternative education was in flower with a whole generation of educators beginning to include mass media and popular culture materials into the classroom (Schrank,

1974). *Man: A Course of Study* (Education Development Center, 1970) was an innovative cross-disciplinary curriculum that used films and simulations for the study of human behavior by elementary and middle school students. The award-winning curriculum was widely used in the United States and won the American Educational Publishers Institute award, an American Film Festival award, two CINE Golden Eagle awards, and a 1971 Emmy Award. Textbooks were beginning to include units on propaganda, persuasion, and advertising, thanks in part to the work of S. I. Hayakawa, who popularized the field of general semantics with his best-selling book *Language in Thought and Action* (Hayakawa, 1949). Although a full historical analysis of the intellectual history of the exploration of media literacy as it developed in the context of secondary English language arts has not yet been conducted, the general tone of these works made clear the idea that advertising exists within a social, historical, economic, and political network which exploits the power of symbols as tools for persuasion.

Many teachers at Concord High School would agree with Douglas Kellner, who has written that the consumer marketplace should be seen as a cultural system and not just as a mechanism for commodities transactions. The cultural symbolism embedded in advertising creates meanings that come to shape consciousness and behavior subtly by sanctioning some forms of thought and behavior while delegitimating others. "Advertising presents proper and improper images of behavior and role models for men and women. The result is a culture where image plays a more important role than linguistic discourse, for while verbal imagery is discursive, visual imagery is nondiscursive, emotional, associative, iconic, and fictive" (Harms & Kellner, 2006, p. 1). Many of the more senior English 11 faculty at Concord High School had had some exposure to these ideas in their own educational backgrounds, and they approached the challenge of exploring advertising, persuasion, and propaganda aware of the intellectual challenge these ideas posed for their students.

BRANDING AND OUR RELATIONSHIP WITH CONSUMER GOODS

With adolescent spending estimated at $170 billion in 2002, marketers know a lot about how to communicate to young people. Many teenagers have come to feel that consumer goods are their friends and that the companies who market to young people are trusted allies (Quart, 2003). As marketing techniques become more and more sophisticated and the lines between marketing, entertainment, and information blur, the topic of brands and branding invites students to consider their own complex emotional relationships with consumer goods.

A number of Concord English 11 teachers acknowledged that students' experiences with advertising were pleasurable. In one in-class writing activity,

Joanne McGlynn asked students to write for 10 minutes about some brands that they're loyal to. Could they list five brands and write about their feelings toward each one? One girl raised her hand and said, "I don't have any brand loyalty." Others nodded. McGlynn said, "OK—just think about it." And then she moved really close and, in a stage whisper, told one girl a personal secret, "I'll tell you one thing: I'll never let a drop of Coke pass my lips." For those students who were struggling with the concept of branding and how brands affect our feelings about products, McGlynn remembers that suddenly their faces lit up and they began to write. After 10 minutes, students groaned when she called time and asked them to stop writing. They complained—they were just getting started on this topic and they had a lot to say. Brand loyalty is deep among this generation of adolescents, and some students celebrate the pleasures of particular brands while others wonder about the power of brands in their lives. According to McGlynn, the discussion that followed this free writing was lively and provocative, with nearly all students participating. By combining the power of free writing to activate students' personal response with a topic as complex as our relationship with branded merchandise, McGlynn found that students were brimming with insights and discoveries. They wanted to talk about how heavy-duty marketing from the cradle onward shapes the social lives of teens, how teens judge one another based on the brands they own, and how objects function symbolically in the construction of personal identity. Through the in-class freewriting activity, students reflected more deeply on how advertising provides pleasure by constructing an association between a human value and a product, situating people in the social role of consumer.

RECOGNIZING THE TARGET AUDIENCE

Joanne McGlynn described another activity that she used with her own favorite magazines including *The New Yorker, Newsweek,* and *Brill's Content.* In small groups, students were given three magazines to analyze. They listed the names of the various products advertised in each magazine, using these lists to generate inferences about the specific demographic characteristics of the target audiences for different magazines. Students could see that *The New Yorker's* ads were very different than those found in *Newsweek,* and they discussed how social class demographics are an important component of segmentation for magazines in the United States. For example, students noticed that the watches advertised in *The New Yorker* were much more expensive than those found in the pages of *Newsweek.* When students found an ad for *Playboy* magazine in *Brill's Content,* they recognized that a large proportion of the target audience for that publication was male. But students complained, "Ms. McGlynn, only a 40-year-old would buy any of these magazines." They wanted to peruse their favorite magazines for this assignment. But McGlynn's philosophy is that it is good for students to encounter media messages in school that they wouldn't normally encounter in the home. "Students are so egocentric. If you give them *Seventeen* and *Sports Illustrated*, that's not going to stretch them."

Adolescence is a time when students are keyed into the concept of individuality and personal identity, while at the same time they are facing enormous social pressures for conformity (Erikson, 1968). Ads are so pervasive in the lives of children and young people that it is "impossible to ignore their wider role in providing people a general education in goods, status, values, social roles, styles and art" (Schudson, 1984, p. 207). Many teenagers may not see themselves as members of a small group that can be described by similarities in gender, race, geography, and social class; however, the process of audience segmentation may influence the development of how adolescents perceive their own personalities. In an experiment involving British teens aged 11 to 14, researchers found that exposure to advertising affected self-reported personality and other psychographic characteristics (Nairn & Berthon, 2005). For some teens, ads that position adolescents as romantic, sex-crazed, wild, or disruptive may encourage young people to view themselves in this way and adopt these behavior qualities. Understanding audience segmentation may help young people recognize how advertising exploits the principle of *social proof*, a concept at the heart of understanding the nature of persuasion and influence. The social proof principle states that people "tend to view a behavior as correct in a given situation to the degree that we see others performing it" (Cialdini, 1988, p. 100).

Advertising makes use of the emotional and cultural values that drive human behavior. Instead of using rational arguments about the benefits of a product, advertisers use symbolism to create emotional bonds between a product and a feeling. As a result, the challenge is to find the "right feeling" to create pathways of desire. Anderson (1995) points out, "To successfully forge emotion/product associations, the ad campaign must ring with authenticity, speaking the language of real people's lives" (p. 76). As Tony Schwartz (1973) explained more than 30 years ago, the most effective ads are the ones with resonance, where consumers recognize some part of themselves.

Because teenagers are frequently the target of advertising that depicts the use of unhealthy products, a deeper appreciation of the concept of audience segmentation is important. English 11 teachers expanded on this topic by purchasing class sets of Jean Kilbourne's *Can't Buy My Love*, the paperback version of *Deadly Persuasion* (1999), a shocking exposé of advertising that shows how ads affect young people, especially girls, by offering false promises of rebellion, connection, and control. The book offers an analysis of the way advertising creates and supports an addictive mentality that often continues throughout adulthood. In Mike Robb Grieco's class, after reading this book, students reflected on how messages about health and lifestyle choices are represented in advertising. Students chose specific social ills that they had concerns about, such as eating disorders, alcoholism, obesity, and drunk driving. Working in small teams, they tore apart magazines to find ads that they believed contributed to the problem. They then used some of the propaganda techniques they had studied to create huge visual messages (on 6" x 8" posters), repurposing the ads they found along with text they arranged, including statistics, provocative comments, and slogans from a variety of sources, including key passages from Kilbourne's book. The giant posters were hung in the public areas of the school. School administrators talked about the feedback they had received from visiting parents and made a visit to the class to personally thank students for creating the posters.

CONSUMPTION AS PLEASURE, CULTURE, AND ENTERTAINMENT

Pleasure and play are a key part of our experience with mass media and popular culture, and some scholars have suggested that in the carnivalesque atmosphere that can sometimes occur when media texts are part of classroom discourse, there is an opportunity to explore issues related to power, identity, and difference (Buckingham, 2003b; Tobin, 2000). Students' obvious pleasure in responding to advertising was sometimes unnerving to the Concord teachers, who generally adopted the position that advertising was a potentially manipulative and dangerous form of communication. Many English 11 teachers were befuddled when their students didn't feel nearly as angry or betrayed as they did about the manipulative strategies advertisers use in persuasion.

When Joanne McGlynn showed students the "Niketown" video from the Canadian video series, *Scanning Television*, students learned about the history and background of this giant entertainment shopping experience, which first opened in Portland in 1990. One method McGlynn used when showing a video in class is to ask students to take careful notes while viewing; she then would select a key passage from the video and ask students to respond or comment on specific arguments and ideas. One day in class, after viewing a segment, McGlynn asked students to comment on a specific key passage: that on a busy day in Chicago, the Niketown store receives 20,000 visitors compared to 3,600 visitors at the Chicago Museum of Art. When McGlynn asked her class, "What does this key passage mean to you?" One student raised his hand and responded very simply, "Art is boring."

McGlynn's face dropped. It wasn't the kind of remark she expected—it was a stunner. She was speechless. It was certainly not her interpretation of the passage. In fact, the student's response was a challenge to the teacher's own beliefs and values, something she didn't want to accept. Yet, in his comment, this teen had captured a perception of contemporary American values that McGlynn herself knew to be true: We are stimulated and entertained not by art, but by the process of consumption. As students responded to this key passage and to the ideas of their peers, the class discussion exploded. Keeping order and encouraging students to listen to others, McGlynn guided the discussion, withholding her own ideas as much as possible and challenging students to articulate their reasoning. As the discussion proceeded, students came to realize that the purpose of the video they had just viewed was not only to inform them about the Niketown store, but rather to stimulate provocative discussion about entertainment and consumption as North American cultural values.   Students were eager to share their thoughts in writing on this challenging topic.

Some of the English 11 faculty engaged students with the question: What are the consequences of a society that values entertainment and consumption above all else? Some (but not all) English 11 teachers used the video from the Media Education Foundation, *Advertising and the End of the World* (1997) which focuses directly on the world of commercial images, asking some basic questions like, Does our consumer society deliver what it claims—happiness and satisfaction? Can we think about our collective as well as our private interests? The video makes the connection between society's high-consumption lifestyle and the coming environmental crisis. Students found the video unnerving because it forced them to evaluate the physical and material costs of life in a consumer society.

Some teachers were troubled by students' unenthusiastic and sometimes negative responses. According to one teacher, "Students didn't find the message as compelling as I did. They didn't all appreciate the feeling of getting one whole hour of the filmmaker's point of view. They kept analyzing the filmmaker's point of view and asking oppositional questions about what was missing." A few English 11 teachers considered this a sign that the curriculum was working—students were being critical thinkers in responding to the video shown in class. These teachers would agree with the conceptualization of media literacy as deeply connected to the cultivation of critical *autonomy,* enabling students to think for themselves. Others were more troubled, feeling dismayed that students didn't accept the political argument at the heart of the video. David Buckingham (2003a) has characterized this as the wish to "impose cultural, moral or political authority" by "colonizing students for their own purposes . . . re-inscribing traditional notions of what counts of knowledge" (p. 314). Scholars like Elizabeth Ellsworth (1997) and Judith Williamson (1981/2) have written about educators' struggles and frustrations with pleasure, identity, and ideology, culminating in the tendency to use media teaching "as a platform to advance our own political and moral positions" (Turnbull, 2003, p. 100). Rather than teach students *what* to think, media literacy educators at Concord High School emphasized teaching students *how* to think, focusing on the importance of exploring questions to ask about the role of media, consumer society, and technology in our lives.

THE POWER OF DIALOGUE

A number of English 11 teachers described other experiences where classroom discussion had veered off in a rich, complex direction as the result of a student's genuine but provocative comment about a topic related to media and communications. Such discussions created an opportunity for a wide range of students to participate, and not only those who had done the reading. These discussions were lively because some of the dominant values of popular culture got placed under the microscope, only to reveal sometimes troubling and uncomfortable insights.

For some English teachers, this kind of discussion represented unfamiliar terrain, not within the "comfort zone" of how teachers perceived the focus of their work. In Martin Nystrand's book, *Opening Dialogue* (1997), the author shows that high school English teachers commonly used monologic genres of classroom discourse, including lecture, recitation, seatwork, and student response to study questions. Nystrand found that highly effective high school English classrooms, however, included a high proportion of engaged dialogue between students and teachers in which "authentic questions challenge students to think and reflect on the consequences of their ideas" and vigorous discussions include the struggle of contradictory opinions, points of view, and value judgments (p. 73).

Several English 11 teachers told me that they sometimes missed the comfort and routine of knowing that on a particular day, they would be on, for example, pages 128 to 150 in the literature reading. Teaching about media and communication didn't work with that kind of predictability because students felt confident to bring their own experiences and knowledge into the classroom. They weren't timid. Despite the latest prescriptions from the ed schools, many teachers like to be the experts—the ones doing most of the talking in the classroom about the topics they care about. But in the English 11 classrooms I observed, students were doing a lot of the talking. Over and over at Concord High School, I saw examples of teachers who were coconstructing meaning through active interpretation of a wide variety of texts, using instructional practices that encourage honest and spontaneous expression and a high level of personal involvement. Students were comfortable and confident while sharing ideas and listening to each others' ideas in response to a particular video excerpt, film, short essay, newspaper article, website, or novel.

Teachers were themselves aware of their "inexpert" status regarding both the specific theoretical content related to media studies and the popular culture texts that students described from their own media consumption at home. As a result, teachers relied on their expertise in using critical questioning and articulation techniques. Students brought their vast knowledge of media culture into the classroom, and teachers helped them develop critical analysis and reflection in examining and questioning their own lived experience. One scholar claims, "The new forms of cultural literacy which can be enabled through media education will only become a reality when . . . teachers learn to listen as well as to talk" (Turnbull, 2003, p. 103). In observing classroom practice, I noticed that teachers were careful not to jump in too quickly to evaluate students' comments and ideas; they let ideas develop and they took students' ideas seriously. Within all the English 11 classrooms I observed, there was a climate of mutual respect and trust. Teachers did not trivialize or demean students' interests in popular culture. Was this respectful climate one of the consequences of heterogeneous grouping? Was it because students were able to activate their genuine expertise as popular culture consumers? Was it the values of the English teachers themselves who seemed universally to recognize that learning happens best when lessons unfold in response to students' ideas and experiences?

Of course, classroom discussions that include an exploration of the values of popular culture are not always upbeat and inspiring from a teacher's point of view. As Bob Cowan put it, "It's easier for me to work with literature than with media. A lot of popular culture does not reinforce the positive values . . . coming from the liberal arts and humanities." When I asked why that was the case, Cowan replied, "Popular culture is who we are, while literature is who we want to be." Despite the challenges of dealing with unfamiliar texts and sometimes uncomfortable topics, Concord teachers trusted themselves to be able to engage students emotionally and intellectually with critical questions. They trusted their students enough to listen to their insights, draw out their ideas, and cultivate their energy to carry the class into rich, complex territory through the process of examining print and media texts that encouraged them to reflect on themselves and their society.

USING LITERATURE TO EXPLORE MECHANISMS OF CULTURAL MANIPULATION

Most English 11 teachers used the literary works *Brave New World, 1984, Fahrenheit 451,* or *Looking Backward 2000–1887* to support student learning aligned with the theme of advertising, propaganda and persuasion. In interviews, teachers told me that they appreciated the chance to deeply explore both fiction and nonfiction works although they were much more comfortable with fiction. Many English 11 teachers were not shy about pointing out their familiarity with helping students read literary texts aesthetically. One teacher described the process by which skillful readers enter into the narrative with their own life experiences in mind, participating in the conflicts, personalities, and situations depicted. Less skillful readers struggle with the meaning-making process, challenged by new vocabulary, shifts in tone and point of view, wrestling with the inference-making required for comprehension. While most of the informational reading in English 11 was accessible in terms of the comprehensibility and overall structure, literary reading uses the power of sustained narrative to pull students in emotionally. English 11 teachers valued the literature selections for Grade 11 because they were more challenging works that invited students to make connections between the present and the past, between various dystopias and utopias. As Mike Robb Grieco explained, "The distance created by fiction, in presenting worlds and characters made for the imagination, allows students a degree of safety not afforded when directly confronting their own real world cultural environments and identities."

Brave New World by Aldous Huxley is one of the most influential novels written in the twentieth century. First published in 1932, Huxley imagined a future world where children are processed genetically in bottles and belong to one of five classes according to their intelligence. In this society, learning takes place by repeating messages during sleep, enforcing certain behavior patterns through suggestion. This is backed up by the legal drug soma that pacifies people through an artificial sense of fulfillment.

Because this unit started with a focus on advertising and contemporary consumer society, even the weakest readers in English 11 were motivated to work hard to dig into Huxley to find the connections. "Lots of students saw the connections between soma and advertising," explained Robb Grieco. Students talked about the social constructs of identity and relationships that are depicted in the book. They actively debated whether the world depicted by Huxley is really the world they're living in today—where advertising has created a population that will always want more, just as in *Brave New World*, where the captive market created by conditioning wanted whatever goods the World State produced. In the book, the culture of constant consumption allowed the Government to act as a supplier, propelling the economy and creating a happy, dependent community. In the twenty-first century, it is the network of global capital that does the same thing. As Jean Baudrillard (1999) has written, consumption is not just the process of individuals satisfying various needs through the purchase of products; it is a system of meaning, like language, based on a code of signs. As a collective behavior, it brings with it a set of values that amount to a kind of indoctrination, since a capitalist society needs both workers and consumers to thrive. "Consumption is therefore a powerful element in social control . . . yet at the same time it requires the intensification of bureaucratic control over the processes of consumption, which is subsequently heralded, with increased intensity, as the reign of freedom" (p. 53).

Video production activities helped students explore the way that propaganda works, giving them a chance to experiment with the uses of images, language, and sound. Heather Ouellette-Cygan included a video production activity as the culminating activity for *Brave New World.* She used the activity developed by a California high school teacher entitled, "Mustapha Mond's Department of Propaganda" (Geib, 2002). Students worked in small groups to create a short video conveying one of these four "public service messages" for the State: (1) shop till you drop; (2) better living through test tubes; (3) never a dull moment; or (4) happiness is a pill. One group created a lively video, resembling a Rollo's candy ad, which featured teens whose problems are solved by means of a soma pill. When a tearful couple are facing a breakup, taking the soma pill cheers them up. When a pedestrian is hit by a car, taking a soma pill makes him forget his injury. Ouellette-Cygan noticed how carefully students worked on the planning process, working collaboratively to write a script and storyboard using catchy jingles and slogans based on their theme. The experience of screening student productions in class intensified the widespread feelings of respect for student creativity, a sensation that the teacher truly enjoyed.

In *Brave New World,* people are treated as objects within the operational logic of supply and demand. Citizens are taught to view one another, and themselves, as commodities to be consumed like any other manufactured goods. Students at Concord High School raised these issues: Isn't this just what we see with celebrities today? They turn themselves into objects in order to make money. And doesn't the very existence of advertising mean that people are not really centered on the commodities themselves?

British critic Raymond Williams (1975) explained that advertising magically associates products with nonmaterialistic and deeply humanistic values, like sex appeal, companionship, love, and social status. More than any other mass media form, ads are shaped to encourage a preferred reading—an interpretation that positions the consumer to adopt a particular attitude towards the product. English 11 teachers, even though many did not use this terminology, were involving students in discussions about advertising that encouraged them to make an oppositional or "nonpreferred" reading (Hall, 1980). Were Concord students generating critical interpretations of advertising because they had learned to ask critical questions and become savvy skeptics or because, having grown up in an oversaturated cultural environment dominated by advertising, they were responding to the formulaic predictability of ads by sarcastically misreading them (Goldman, 1992)? Regardless, responding to literature that invited them to consider the nature of propaganda and its power as a mechanism of social control certainly contributed to the development of students' critical analysis skills.

Many English 11 teachers screened *Wag the Dog* (1997) to explore the topic of media manipulation in relationship to government power. In discussing the film after having the students read Orwell's 1984, English 11 teacher Michael Robb Grieco downplayed the direct political/satirical connection to contemporary politics in favor of focusing on the propaganda techniques elaborately demonstrated by the spin doctors in the film. He encouraged students to recognize the film as a form of political satire. But he also focused the discussion on what the film reveals about the process of selecting, organizing, and developing ideas that work as forms of propaganda.

To provide balance to what some English 11 teachers considered to be a deterministic and depressing perspective on culture, some assigned a challenge novel, Edward Bellamy's *Looking Backward 2000–1887* (1888/2003), a best-selling book of the nineteenth century that provides a critique of industrial capitalism while describing a utopian vision of the future. In this novel, the narrator is transported into the future and finds that the economy is based on publicly owned capital. The government controls the means of production and divides the national product equally between all citizens. Every citizen receives a college-level education. Individuals are given a great deal of freedom in choosing a career, and everyone retires at the age of 45. Society is based on an ideal of the brotherhood of man, and it is unthinkable that any individual should suffer the evils of poverty or hunger. While *Looking Backward* also looks critically at consumer society, Bellamy's novel invited students to consider the future as malleable and open to change. English 11 teacher Christine Oskar-Poisson developed a creative writing assignment where students could invent their own utopias, explaining their reasons for forming a utopia and describing the characteristics of the new society.

In debating the consequences of life in a consumer society, some students found much to celebrate, and others had concerns about whether they were truly as free as they had previously imagined. People like to possess beautiful and useful objects, but it's not the exclusive goal of life, one student explained. People like to think that having objects will "fix" them in some way—and what's wrong with believing that even if it's not true? But consumption as a requirement is not really freedom, pointed out one student. It's not the government enslaving people like in *Brave New World*, another student pointed out. Another wondered, is it any different if it's big corporations?

A few English 11 teachers used *1984* with English 11 students to explore the theme of language and power. In this classic novel, George Orwell described a totalitarian society in which the government, referred to as the Party, had almost complete control over the people. The supreme ruler of the Party was Big Brother. Posters announced that "Big Brother Is Watching You." Telescreens

droned endlessly with brainwashing propaganda about government progra
Coins, stamps, books, films, and banners proclaimed the three slogans of the
Party: War is Peace, Freedom is Slavery, and Ignorance is Strength. In *1984,*
Orwell sounds an alarm against the abusive nature of authoritarian governments,
examining the psychology of power and the ways that manipulations of language
and history can be used as mechanisms of control.

With *1984,* English 11 teachers were skillful in using literature to open
up conversation about words and how they work. In the dystopian society,
the B-vocabulary words were compound words, merged together in an easy
pronounceable form, like "goodthink." Many of the B-words were euphemisms
like "joycamp" (forced labor camp). Some words were ambivalent, having a
positive connotation when applied to the Party, and a bad connotation when
applied to its enemies. In responding to a writing prompt requiring a five-
paragraph essay about the power of language in contemporary society, one of
Val Aubry's students wrote:

> Word choice has long been a device for powerful and persuasive
> communication. Every word has a connotation: similar words can imply
> totally different things. The words "childish" and "childlike" are a good
> example of this. These words are very closely related, but "childish" has
> the connotation of immature while "childlike" has a connotation of
> having a younger appearance. While watching, reading, or looking at any
> form of media, one needs to think about the biases and politics behind
> the media and how they influenced word and image selection.

Advertising saturates the cultural environment of the adolescent and
provides a form of socialization that shapes social attitudes and behaviors.
At Concord High School, teachers brought their own perspectives on the
ideological dimensions of advertising, persuasion, and propaganda into their
classrooms, emphasizing key themes that revolved around the pleasures of
consumption, brand loyalty and socialization, the role of consumer goods in
the development of cultural values, and the dangers associated with global
capitalism. Literary selections helped students comfortably inhabit, observe,
and criticize without directly confronting their own reality or risking the
security of their own identities. Capitalizing on the power of dialogue to
transform the teaching and learning process, classroom discussion centered on
the relationship between the individual and the state, the meaning of "freedom,"
and the role of language and images in structuring our conceptualizations of
social reality—past, present, and future.

Chapter 5

Issues of Representation

In James Doneski's English 11 class, the topic was gender representations in the mass media. The assignment: Boys had to choose a TV show from a list of shows targeting women, and girls had to choose a TV show from a list of shows targeting men. Students then had to watch one episode of that show three times and write about how their own gender was being portrayed, examining the characters, plots, and themes. Students choosing to take on the "challenge" level were invited to also examine the commercials that aired during the show and write about patterns of gender stereotyping in the ads.

Doneski had handed out a list of popular television shows, mostly sitcoms and dramas from network television, organized into two columns. One column included shows that primarily appeal to young women, like *Sabrina the Teenage Witch*, a sitcom featuring the wholesome adventures of a teen witch and her family; *Sister Sister*, a drama focused on the lives of two sisters who were formerly separated but later rejoined; and *Felicity*, a drama about a young woman who abandons the chance to go to college at Stanford and follows her boyfriend to college in New York City. Another column listed shows that young men liked to watch in the late 1990s, including *Millennium*, a FOX network show from the creators of *The X-Files*, which centered on psychic and FBI profiler Frank Black, who tracks down violent criminals; *Seven Days*, a UPN network show about a former CIA agent who travels back in time to stop a terrorist attack on the president of the United States; *Law and Order: Special Victims Unit*, a gritty detective drama featuring the investigation of sex crimes; and *Sports Night*, an ABC comedy/drama about people who work at a television station.

In order to prepare students for this assignment, Doneski assigned students some reading—short essays from Steven Stark's book, *Glued to the Set* (1997) and other nonfiction short articles he found on the Internet. After reading, students discussed what they had learned about the changing patterns of gender representation in shows from TV history, including *Ozzie and Harriet*, *All in the Family*, and *The Mary Tyler Moore Show*. In class, they viewed and discussed *Dreamworlds* (1995), a film that explores the representation of women on music videos. "I'm trying to encourage students to think on a metacognitive level," explained Doneski. "When I met them in September, they would just sit in front of the TV and consume." At the heart of the course, he explained, is the idea of supporting students as critical thinkers and active interpreters, strengthening their ability to generate ideas and compose messages.

This chapter presents some of the instructional practices that English 11 teachers used to promote an understanding of the concept of representation, including activities in which students explored historical patterns of representation evident through television's depiction of American culture; the use of race and gender stereotypes; the depiction of the "other" in film and literature; and the political economy of representation. The topic of representation matters because adolescents benefit from understanding how the images, stories, and patterns of identity are presented to them as "natural" through TV comedy and drama. For students in Doneski's class, how men and women behave in the stories on television wasn't something they ordinarily would pay attention to or discuss. But the concept of representation helped students see how entertainment media convey cultural values and norms. Doneski's writing assignment forced students to look closely at television shows as a type of text with a specific world view. The learning experience raised new questions for them about the network of socially constructed roles that they are participating in as adolescents. "They will leave this course with the ability to ask questions," said Doneski assuredly, "even though they may not receive any easy answers to the questions we explore."

WHAT IS REPRESENTATION?

All media texts are "re-presentations" of reality. As one of the key concepts of media literacy, students learn that messages are intentionally composed, written, framed, cropped, and created by people who are involved in constructing a message for a specific purpose, and that media messages represent some aspects of lived experience (Manoff & Schudson, 1986; McLuhan, 1964). All media forms, from science fiction TV shows to a home video to a glossy magazine, are representations of someone's concept of existence, codified into a series of signs and symbols which can be read by an audience. The concept of *representation* is rooted in the field of semiotics, the study of symbol systems (Barthes, 1972; Chandler, 2002; Hall, 1980). Scholars from the fields of linguistics, media studies, and communication examine the complex relationship between symbols and what they stand for. Because images resemble the things they represent, philosophers have argued that visual symbols possess some of the properties of the object represented. For example, Umberto Eco (1976) explains how photographs and images may reproduce some of the features of real objects, but only some of them. An image of a zebra may be recognized by the stripes alone, without noticing the exact shape of the head, for example. As Messaris (1994) writes, images "reproduce many of the informational cues that people make use of in their perception of physical and social reality" (p. 165). While people sometimes talk about how children and young people need to learn the grammar of reading images, it's not an accurate description of the cognitive processes involved in interpreting images. Very little learning is required to understand the compositional elements of photographs or the editing conventions of film and television. Studies have shown that people without any experience with film or visual media can understand the editing techniques that manipulate point of view and time order (Hobbs, Stauffer, Frost, & Davis, 1988). Visual images derive their power from the fact that humans use the same cognitive skills in reading them as they use in everyday perception, so we process media representations as if they were actual reality.

Media representations extend our perceptions of reality, giving us symbolic access to people, ideas, and information that are beyond the limitations of our direct real-world experience. For example, I'm only rarely in Washington, D.C., but I receive many ideas about what happens there every day from watching TV news, reading the newspaper, and even from reading novels and seeing fictional films that feature politics and government as a setting. Without media texts, my understanding of Washington would be very limited. Figure 5.1 shows a model of how the concept of representation can be understood as a key dimension of the processes of both writing and reading. Authors (whether they're writing fiction, shooting a documentary video, or composing an informational web page) compose texts with an understanding of how their messages exist in relation to their lived experiences, and audiences assess texts using their perceptions of the texts' relationship to their own lived experiences. Audiences are vulnerable to manipulation because in most situations, they are not able to directly or independently assess the relationship between a media text and the actuality it may claim to represent (Alvarado & Boyd-Barrett, 1992; Nichols, 1991; 1981). Every time I view a wildlife documentary, or read about political events in a country on the other side of the world, or watch a movie about a historical event, I gain some ideas about some aspect of life on this planet. But because the author has made choices about what to emphasize and what to omit in constructing the text, my experience is restricted. Only the dramatic moments of animal behavior in the woods of Montana are portrayed in that wildlife documentary; editors and journalists make decisions about which aspects of the news events will be highlighted and which aspects will be ignored; and movie producers telescope historical events and expand historical personalities to fit the storytelling requirements for action, romance, and conflict. That's why English 11 teachers made such active use of

Figure 5.1. The Concept of Representation.

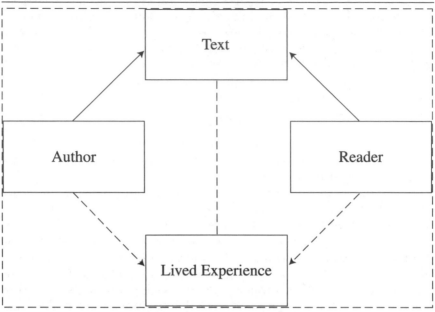

Note. Adapted from Bazalgette (1992).

the cultural question, "What is omitted from this message?" The question of omissions opens up opportunities to explore patterns of representation.

Faced with the complexity of the concept of representation, some students are likely to reflect cynically that all media messages are fiction—with no relationship to reality. But since we inevitably base our perception of reality on the media messages that surround us, that simple solution is not really an option. The topic of representation must be a central concept for understanding both the processes of authorship and message reception in all forms of symbolic expression.

MEDIA REPRESENTATIONS: PAST, PRESENT, AND FUTURE

English 11 teacher Val Aubry began her focus on representation by asking students to read short essays in Steven Stark's *Glued to the Set* (1997), a review of sixty television shows that traces the evolution of the medium and its effects on individuals and society, with each chapter devoted to critical analysis of one particular show (including *Entertainment Tonight*, *Sesame Street*, and *Roseanne*). Elements of current television programming can be seen in some of the shows created back in the 1960s and 1970s. For example, shows like *The Dating Game* and *The Gong Show* held the seeds of tabloid television, reality shows, and their exhibitionistic culture of confession. Stark shows how television programs present radical or threatening social ideas using comedy, in shows like *All in the Family* and *M*A*S*H*. Most of the essays in *Glued to the Set* emphasize two key points: First, most American TV shows conform to a powerful ethos to make advertising look good; shows that contradict the spirit of consumerism have less of a chance of making it to television. Second, prime-time network entertainment tends to be designed for a stressed-out audience watching at home without paying much attention. Television's programming structure is intentionally designed to be understood even if you leave the room, listen from another room, or even miss parts of the show while channel surfing (Kakutani, 1997).

After reading some of these essays and discussing them as a large group, many English 11 teachers had students work in teams to select one particular program from the 1960s or the 1970s and compose a research report by conducting library research using the Internet. Aubry created an assignment rubric that identified the specific information students needed to gather, including the program genre, a description of the characters, the name of the producer, the scheduling history, historical background, audience appeal, and awards. Students had to identify what kinds of values and themes were explored and how the show broke new ground culturally or technologically. Students created a timeline of the decade when the television show was aired and gathered information about the political and cultural events that took place during that same time period. Each person made an oral presentation describing what they learned. Even though it was not required, several students put together short excerpts of the shows which they had taped off the air so that they could show certain features of the shows or characters depicted. Working collaboratively, class members then created an outline of trends they noticed through the decades.

Aubry recalls, "For kids who normally have a hard time with school, some of them just took off on this. We had an amazing discussion about the representation of sex on television when we talked about *The Dating Game*." English 11 students were fascinated to learn from their library research that the real idea behind *The Dating Game* was to see how much sex talk could be gotten away with without getting in trouble with the network's standards and practices division. The show was crammed with loaded questions ("Bachelor Number One: If I were an ice cream cone, would you lick my cream or bite my cone?") and coy, yet revealing, answers. "For some students, this was their first real experience with the thrill of research," explained Aubry, "where they were finding information not just because it was part of a required assignment, but because they were genuinely interested in the topic." After the presentations,

Aubry led students, as a large group, through the creation of a chart explicitly comparing and contrasting all the shows students had investigated. Her purpose was to highlight some of the ways in which television was continually revising its representations of different aspects of lived experience, and in the process both simultaneously reflecting and shaping American cultural values. Students had a hard time imagining that certain shows had really been controversial during the eras in which they had aired. They talked about how their parents' interpretations of these shows were sometimes different from their own perspectives, and recognized that texts exist within multiple historical contexts and must be read with sensitivity to those contexts.

REPRESENTATIONS OF THE MONSTER

A number of English 11 teachers used *Frankenstein* (Shelley, 1818/1994) to explore the themes of the consequences of the quest for knowledge, the concept of the other as monster, and issues of representation as they relate to the way the monster is depicted across multiple time periods. When Mary Shelley first published *Frankenstein* in 1818, it opened the door for a new genre, science fiction. The story centers on young Victor Frankenstein and his obsession with creating life. But upon seeing the grotesqueness of his creation, Frankenstein flees it. The creature, however, futilely seeks to find acceptance among humans, and in the end both the creator and the creature are destroyed.

English 11 teacher Val Aubry fondly remembers the surprise of some students when they read the book and discovered early on that Frankenstein was the name of the creator, not the name of the monster he created. She started the unit by inviting students to wonder why this particular story and its themes have inspired so many other stories, including books, TV shows, and films. Right before students got to the chapter where the monster is created, Aubry invited them to pay special attention to the scene in the novel where the monster is "born." She showed them a scene from *Frankenstein* (1931), the classic film featuring Boris Karloff as the bolt-headed monster.

According to Aubry, students came in the next day saying, "Well, I thought the birth of the monster was going to really be something dramatic, but it was just a paragraph." They then looked closely at that paragraph, reflecting on the choices Shelley made in describing the scene. Aubry then invited students to notice the similarities and differences in how the monster's creation is depicted in two newer versions of the story, using brief clips from *Young Frankenstein* (1974), a parody version featuring Gene Wilder as Victor Frankenstein, and *Mary Shelley's Frankenstein* (1994), with Robert DeNiro as the monster in a film that retells the story as Mary Shelley originally created it. She remembers the questions that came up in class: Why are these scenes so different from each other and from the novel? What was Mary Shelley's point in not emphasizing this particular scene? Probing the text more deeply, many students began to feel that Mary Shelley really wasn't putting major emphasis on technology and science as the means of creation; instead, they believed her primary focus was the father–son relationship, the metaphor of birth, and its relationship to the nature of human empathy. From a twenty-first century perspective, contemporary readers can't help but view the "birth" of the monster as an allegory about how the dangers and excesses of technology and science enable us to lose touch with our humanity. But Shelley was the daughter of a prominent protofeminist. Viewed from the nineteenth century, students learned that the story seemed to speak about the mysteries and obligations of parenting, love, identity, and autonomy.

Students also examined the structure of the book, recognizing that the story is presented from the point of view of Robert Walton, the sea captain who meets Dr. Frankenstein; then from the point of view of the creator of the monster, Victor Frankenstein; and finally from the point of view of the creature. Students appreciated how the presentation of a story from multiple points of view involves the reader in "filling in the gaps," noticing what is emphasized and what is omitted. For example, students noticed that when the monster describes his killing, he does it in a very nonchalant way, which indicates his lack of empathy and sense of moral responsibility.

Aubry then invited students to consider the question: How does the representation of the monster reflect the historical context of the time period? She gave students a book review of *Monster Theory*, edited by Jeffrey Cohen (1996), a set of essays that explore the idea that each culture and time period creates monsters that reflect the anxieties of that community. Aubry explained, "Just as Mary Shelley's novel can be read in terms of her world view at a time when views about men's and women's social roles were shifting, the 1931 film version of *Frankenstein* can be read in terms of people's fears about the Depression. When we're not afraid of those same things anymore, they become comical. But then we create new monsters." In responding to the book review, students talked about all the new monsters—aliens, terrorists, government, and technology.

Bob Cowan and James Doneski also used *Frankenstein* to explore issues related to power and technology as they shape human relationships. Doneski worded his focus question this way: "How are monsters a representation of both our culture and ourselves?" Cowan's outline of the questions and issues that served to focus his study of the novel is shown in Figure 5.2. He wanted students to reflect on how the characters and ideas in the novel reflect the time period; how the novel's representation of the creature compares to the popular

Figure 5.2. Questions for *Frankenstein*.

Pre-Unit Questions

1. Describe the Frankenstein monster in looks and personality. Draw a sketch of the monster.
2. As a child, when did you first hear about the Frankenstein monster? How old were you?
3. Why do you think the Frankenstein monster is so well known? Why do monsters fascinate us?
4. Do you think people are born innocent and they become corrupt as they grow up, or do you believe that we have evil born into us? Explain your point of view.
5. What have you read or heard about Mary Shelley's Frankenstein?

Essential Unit Questions

To be successful in this unit, read about, jot down notes and key passages, discuss in class, and expect to think and write on these questions:

6. How do the characters and ideas in this novel reflect the time period (historical context) during which it was published?
7. How does the original novel about the Frankenstein monster compare to and contrast with the vision and understanding of the monster you had before you read? How do you explain these differences?
8. What does this novel teach us about human nature and how it is influenced by society?
9. All media messages have embedded values. What does this novel teach us about technology and human nature?
10. Similarly, what does did this author want us to respect and value?
11. Based on this novel, what is a monster? Define the term. Based on this novel, what can we learn from monsters?
12. What is an archetype? What archetypes are symbolized in this novel?
13. What symbols of hope, decency, and justice can we find in this novel?

Questions of Fact

14. Who are the main characters and what do they value in life?
15. What are the main conflicts in this novel?
16. According to Freud, what are the three parts of human personality, and what are the three levels of consciousness?

Questions of Style

17. What is dramatic irony, and what are two examples of this literary device in this novel?
18. What is poetic justice? What is one primary example of it in the novel?

Note. Developed by Bob Cowan.

culture version of the monster; what the novel has to say about technology and human values; and how symbolism is used.

James Doneski liked how he was able to layer various kinds of challenge activities into the curriculum, especially to promote student reading and analysis skills. He estimated that about half of the students in his class struggled with fluency and comprehension as they responded to literary texts. All students used at least one common text during each unit in Doneski's class. For the unit on the monster, he explained, "My challenge kids will read *Frankenstein* more quickly because they can, and then they'll go off and read something else, like a critical essay I found on the topic of gothic genres." The process worked this way: during a unit, Doneski offered various challenge activities, and different students were free to take on those challenges. Generally, challenge activities were de rigeur for the high-ability college-bound students in his class. Doneski remembered being surprised and pleased that some challenge activities appealed to students who were not the usual participants, in part because heterogeneous grouping tends to encourage all students to perform to the best of their ability. Media literacy activities may be especially beneficial in heterogeneous classrooms because they create rich learning opportunities for students whose reading comprehension skills may not be as strong as their overall intellectual ability.

GENDER, RACE, AND STEREOTYPES IN THE MEDIA

Only a small number of teachers at Concord High School explicitly addressed the issues of race, stereotypes, and representation. New Hampshire is one of the least racially diverse states in the United States with fewer than 1% of the population African American, 2% Asian, and 2% Hispanic (U.S. Bureau of the Census, 1995). Mike Robb Grieco explored the topic of racial representation using essays from *Glued to the Set* (Stark, 1997). After reading selected essays on shows from the 1970s, Robb Grieco screened brief excerpts from a 2-hour CBS show on television shows from the 1970s to explore the way that stereotyping is used in television programming. In discussing the program, "Students were shocked at the way race was presented in shows of that time period," Robb Grieco recalled. "We used Silverblatt's keys to media literacy to understand how entertainment media shape the social and cultural realities and values of a society." These concepts include *process*, which includes the function of a particular message, the author, and the audience; *context*, which includes a focus on history, culture, and structure; *framework*, which refers to various structural elements of a production, including plot and genre; and *production values*, which includes editing, color, lighting, sound, and other elements (Silverblatt, 1995).

At the conclusion of this unit, Robb Grieco asked students to write essays on a specific media text reflecting on the use of stereotypes. One Korean student wrote about racial stereotypes in *The Wayans Brothers*, a situation comedy that used exaggerated physical comedy as the main comedic element rather than character-driven conflicts and witty dialogue. Another student looked at stereotypes of overweight people on *The Drew Carey Show* and talked about the show's tendency to use comedy in ways that both reinforced and challenged fat stereotypes. For example, the student described the character of Mimi Brobeck, who is a smart-mouthed, hostile, fat woman who wears bright colors and circus-clown-inspired makeup. The show examined weight issues in a series of episodes, showing in a realistic way how overweight affects people's sense of self-esteem.

Robb Grieco was impressed with the creative way in which students made use of the concept of stereotypes in writing their essays. Their descriptive writing was strong because students were writing about their personal interests; they felt a need to explain their ideas clearly because they cared about the shows they had selected. Their analytic writing was effective because students were able to make use of the concepts provided in the classroom in structuring their own writing and thinking and apply them to topics they knew well.

DISCOURSE COMMUNITIES AND REPRESENTATION

Mike Robb Grieco also asked students to keep a Media Journal, reflecting on their experiences consuming media and the insights they gained from the class discussions. He used this writing activity as a means to encourage students to broaden their reading about topics related to the course and reflect upon their media use at home. When the class turned to exploring stereotypes in the media, a student we'll call Sarah began her entry with "I don't feel comfortable discussing race. I don't think I know enough on the subject. I could be one of those people who are 'not even aware of subtle prejudices that shape their view of the world.'" This student was responding to an article she had found in the *Boston Globe* entitled "Skin Tones and Racial Stereotyping" (Cook, 2002). After reading it, she became aware of her previously unconscious stereotypes about race. About being prejudiced, she wrote, "In fact, I really think I am, not by choice. It was just picked up along the way." Robb Grieco recognized that many students in Concord shared prejudiced attitudes about African Americans and other minorities. In his ambitious unit to explore representation, Robb Grieco introduced students to some basic language of sociolinguistics and discourse theory, including concepts like *dialect, discourse community, language variety, speech acts,* and *identity*. He had been deeply influenced by his reading of James Paul Gee and Michel Foucault as a graduate student in education at the University of New Hampshire. Critical discourse analysis is a contemporary approach to the study of language and discourses in social institutions, looking at how social relationships, identity, knowledge, and power are constructed through written and spoken texts in communities, schools and classrooms (Gee, 2004).

Using the film *Six Degrees of Separation* (1993), Robb Grieco's English 11 students discussed the character of Paul, played by Will Smith, who was a destitute African American street hustler who gained access and acceptance into the wealthy society of New Yorkers through a contrived comembership in the discourse communities of a particular White wealthy couple. After viewing the film, Robb Grieco and his students worked through the creation of a discourse identity map, detailing the various discourse communities through which Paul found comembership or alienation. Students then created their own discourse identity maps, showing the various discourse communities that they held membership in. He invited students to list the various symbols (common topics of discussion, activities, and other signifiers) for each discourse community. Figure 5.3 shows an example of a writing prompt that the teacher used to explore this issue.

This activity helped develop a feeling of safety among students as they delved into complex and personal issues of social class and identity, according to Robb Grieco. "It's important that students extend their comfort zones and develop an increased ability to be curious about what they don't yet know. Media literacy's practice of asking questions can offer students more opportunity to extend their personal power. When done well, the balance of students' feelings should shift toward being comfortable with being curious and engaged." After reflecting on their discourse identity maps, students were able to increase their own respect for others in the class and value the diversity of perspectives that were present among the heterogeneous groups of adolescents.

When it was time to read the students' Media Journals after the unit on representation had concluded, Robb Grieco was jolted as he read Sarah's latest entry. Only a few weeks after the unit had ended, she had written: "After our discussion last week I really felt good. It was so stirring to hear how interested the class was. Almost everyone shared a good point and those who didn't speak were hooked by others' contagious words. I was interested in taking an African American History class when I go to college and now I know I will take one." In reflecting on the power of the concept of representation to help students recognize how their identity is situated within a network of power relationships, Robb Grieco said, "I have witnessed students grow more critically aware, more intellectually curious, and more expressive."

In some situations, English 11 teachers were not completely comfortable exploring issues of representation related to gender, race, and social class. In one case, Bob Cowan wanted students to see how media texts worked in terms of their own identity formation, socialization, and childhood experiences.

Figure 5.3. A Writing Prompt to Explore Discourse Identity Maps.

After viewing the film *Six Degrees of Separation,* respond to A or B and C by writing the prompt and completing the tasks listed below the prompt in paragraph form.

A. One way Paul earned the Kiddriches' trust was through communicating an apparent comembership in a discourse community revolving around...

- name the discourse community of your choice
- detail the content (jargon, vocabulary, references, topics, themes, concerns, values)
- offer specific examples from the film of various forms of communication that show membership (describe themes of pronunciation, inflection, appearances, physicality, etc)

B. One way Paul earned the Utah couple's trust was through communicating an apparent co-membership in a discourse community revolving around...

- name the discourse community of your choice
- detail the content (jargon, vocabulary, references, topics, themes, concerns, values)
- offer specific examples from the film of various forms of communication that show membership (describe themes of pronunciation, inflection, appearances, physicality, etc)

C. I connect with (name the members of the discourse community—friends, coworkers, teammates, family) through comembership in a discourse community revolving around...

- detail the content (jargon, vocabulary, references, topics, themes, concerns, values)
- offer specific examples from your life experience of the various forms of communication that show membership (describe themes of pronunciation, inflection, appearances, physicality, etc)

Note. Developed by Michael Robb Grieco.

Early in the school year, after defining *mass media* to include film, newspapers, TV shows, magazines, radio, popular music, video games, and the Internet, he asked students to create a mass media timeline going back to their earliest childhood. What media texts did students remember from their preschool years? From elementary school? From middle school? Students were asked to identify some of the media texts they remembered from their childhood, create a timeline, draw a picture or use an image, and write one sentence about each text describing what was memorable about each one. Cowan recalls, "We went around the room, and students shared one sentence and then informally elaborated on a particular media text. There was a very clear distinction along gender lines. The violent proclivities or tendencies of the male viewers came hard up against the girls who were looking at film and reflecting about life and relationships. It was real eye-opener. And I wasn't able to capitalize or develop that. And I really would have been half afraid to."

As a veteran teacher, Cowan is aware of how gender differences may affect student learning. He has seen how his English 11 students gravitate toward gender-based friendships in both school tasks and other activities. He has observed that boys are more likely than girls to call out answers but that girls are more responsible in getting assignments completed. He actively uses deliberate orchestration of mixed gender groups to create opportunities for boys and girls to work together; he sometimes assigns specific jobs within groups to avoid students gravitating toward stereotypical roles. Cowan is aware of how his own attitudes about media representations and gender have been shaped by his own cultural expectations and social class—he has strong opinions about violence in video games and on television; he is deeply concerned about the many media texts that are targeted to young men and promote or justify violence as a legitimate means of problem solving.

But in this particular learning experience, the topic of gender emerged rather unexpectedly and Cowan wasn't ready for the topic. For the personal media timeline activity, his goals were not focused on the topic of gender representation per se—his aim for this lesson was to invite students to reflect on media's role in the life of an individual. Although he wanted to be able to address the issue of violent masculinity with sensitivity, he felt it was too early in the term to begin to dig in and analyze students' highly gendered media preferences. He was afraid of the unpredictability of the topic, especially with a group of adolescents whom he was just beginning to get to know. At this point in the semester, Cowan was still actively working to establish a culture of trust in his classroom, and he recognized that the topic of gender may have polarized the classroom at a time when he was actively encouraging students to build trust and mutual respect within the peer group. The time for this topic was just not right. Later in the semester, when Cowan moved into his unit on advertising, he did include a special focus on analyzing representations of women and men in the media.

THE ECONOMICS OF REPRESENTATION

When English 11 teachers selected Carl Hiaasen's *Team Rodent* (1998) for inclusion as a nonfiction text, they especially appreciated its topic (the Disney Company), its tone (scathingly funny) and its length (83 pages). The book addresses a serious and complex subject on the theme of representation: the ability of power to create its own reality. In the late 1990s this same theme was prominent in the early *X-Files* episodes and the film *The Truman Show*. It was a claim that linked the topic of representation with that of media economics (Taylor, 1998). For children and young people, it's not an overstatement to say that Disney's media culture has become "a substantial educational force in regulating the meanings, values, and tastes that set the norms," offering up and legitimating particular social roles—what it means to claim "identity as male, female, white, black, citizen, noncitizen, adult or child" (Giroux, 1999, pp. 2–3).

Teachers of writing and composition who have used critiques of Disney to promote reading, writing, and the development of critical literacy have noted how students resist a critical perspective of a beloved icon. Virginia Crank (2005) wrote about how her freshmen college students responded to her use of Disney critique as a means to promote students' critical reading and response:

> [Student] resistance emerges partly from the cognitive dissonance created by challenging deeply held notions of childhood and children's entertainment, and their response to the dissonance is an insistence that our critiques of culture do not matter. In their frustration, they say things like, "Why do we even have to talk about this? We're not going to change Disney by talking about it in this class." They feel, in some sense, that their voices have no power in the culture, and that writing about such ideas doesn't matter because it does not produce immediate, direct results. (p. 1)

Like the students described in this passage, Concord High School students were genuinely floored by the arguments and ideas in their reading of *Team Rodent*. Since birth, Concord English teachers reckoned, they and their students had been participating in various material aspects of Disney culture, which all deliver the mantra, "Disney is good." *Team Rodent* gave them a perspective on Disney that was completely antithetical to every media representation they had previously encountered about the well-known media firm.

Team Rodent represents the Disney Company as the megacorporation it is, with $25 billion in annual revenues coming from films, television, home video and stage plays, radio and TV stations, theme parks on three continents, computer software, toys and merchandise, sports teams and hotels, real estate holdings, shopping centers and retail stores, housing developments and even a cruise line. Every American gets a big dose of Disney. According to Hiaasen, that is rapidly becoming true as well in France, Spain, Germany, Japan, Great Britain, Scandinavia, Australia, China, Mexico, Brazil, and Canada. As media companies control more and more of the cultural communications landscape, they can present representations and worldviews that conform to a single vision. Disney's media products emphasize a comforting worldview where heroes and villains are clearly demarcated and all endings are happy.

English 11 teachers themselves held a variety of perspectives on Disney as a cultural phenomenon. They didn't stand on a soapbox and coax students into hating Disney. Instead, they enjoyed the opportunity to have students get riled up by their reading—it's something that doesn't occur that often in English literature classes. After the students read *Team Rodent,* some English 11 teachers invited students to reflect and analyze the feelings they experienced when encountering a media representation that profoundly contradicts numerous previously encountered media representations.

Why is it so uncomfortable to encounter ideas that challenge our assumptions? From a cognitive information-processing perspective, people seek consistency. We prefer to consume media messages that do not challenge our existing belief systems because it makes information processing more efficient (Potter, 2004). Media representations reaffirm our understanding of social reality. That's why conservative Republicans prefer watching FOX News and liberal Democrats prefer listening to National Public Radio. In managing the complex overload of representations that we are flooded with, we simplify whenever possible by avoiding messages that don't require a full-fledged engagement with complexity. Media stereotypes feed into people's coping strategies with dealing with the symbol-rich representational environment that is a ubiquitous part of contemporary life. English 11 teachers were confident enough in their goals of exploring the concept of representation to promote critical reading, writing, and thinking that they could challenge students' existing beliefs.

REPRESENTATIONS, PLEASURE, AND THE DEVELOPMENT OF PERSONAL IDENTITY

Media representations derive their power partly from the fact that we spend large parts of our lives consuming them and partly because we invest large amounts of emotional and psychic energy as a result of the pleasures we derive from them. Mike Robb Grieco used a series of activities that enabled students to consider how media representations both reflect and shape their sense of personal and social identity. To examine in more depth the role of popular culture in the development of personal identity, he screened and discussed *High Fidelity* (2000), a film adaptation of the book by Nick Hornsby featuring John Cusack and Jack Black. The film explores the life of a young man working at a record store. Reflecting on his failed love life, he considers the role of music in shaping his expectations about romantic relationships and his own priorities in life. His immersion in pop music has resulted in a loss of human connection. For example, when his ex-girlfriend's father dies, he creates a list of the top five pop songs about death (including "Leader of the Pack" and "Dead Man's Curve"). For the characters in the film, death is merely "pop song fodder, like love and everything else." As the film develops, the main character understands that the texts of popular music have made him who he is and that, to continue his development as an adult, he must move from being a "professional appreciator" toward more active involvement in creating music and participating in the recording industry. Most important, he learns to respect the cultural preferences of others whose taste in music is different from his own (Reinsch, 2006).

After viewing the film, the teacher asked students to create their own "Top Five" list of songs. Which songs are most important to you and why? Students were asked to make a 5-minute speech and play 5 minutes of music in responding to this question. One young woman had been to visit her relatives in India the previous summer and talked about how, in India, music was more than just a commodity to consume. She played music she found on the soundtrack of the film, *Monsoon Wedding*, and talked about how music functions as a communal participatory experience in the daily lives of women in rural India. Another student talked about the songs that his dad loved, and described his connection to his father through those songs. He never gets to hear those songs anymore since his parents divorced. Through sharing songs and discussing their personal meanings, students learn how media texts are a key dimension of our own lived experiences, identities, and social relationships. The media representations we consume extend symbolically far beyond what the author may have intended to express. In providing feelings of pleasure that are unique because of the active position they hold in our day-to-day lives, we are constantly engaged in "textual poaching," creating meanings that are personal and idiosyncratic because they are accompanied by emotional involvement (Jenkins, 1992). By inviting students to reflect on the consequences of their own choices as media consumers and to be curious about the media choices made by others, English 11 teachers were helping students create a learning community that assumed high levels of engagement and participation.

In this chapter, I have shown how exploring issues of representation supported growth in students' metacognitive skills, encouraging them to reflect on their own thinking processes and consider how media and technologies convey values, norms, and expectations. A deeper understanding of representation leads students away from being cynical because they appreciate the decision-making processes involved in constructing messages. The theoretical lens of representation provides a framework for each student to evaluate how various types of texts (in literature, expository texts, visual and electronic media) relate to lived experience; repeated opportunities to apply this framework help students become comfortable in evaluating the authenticity and quality of the messages they receive. This perspective also works for students as writers and composers of media messages, as they consider how, through their choices of image, language, music and other symbol systems, they are shaping messages in ways that reflect their own value systems and life experiences.

Students' appreciation of literature was enriched by opportunities to explore how literary texts exist within historical contexts, and that they need to be read with sensitivity to those contexts. For many students at Concord High School, their reading of literature in English 11 was not just a matter of the routine practice of "find the theme, motif, and symbols and crank out the essay." Students discovered that readers are part of a discourse community: Our own reading practices are situated within a network of contemporary cultural assumptions, and these assumptions shape the way we read and interpret works of literature, news media, movies, websites, and popular culture. This insight stimulated rich learning opportunities for students whose reading comprehension may not be as strong as their overall ability, and students' descriptive and analytic writing improved as a result of providing a critical framework that connected contemporary cultural media products to classic texts.

In the next part of this book, Measuring Media Literacy, I document some of the many learning outcomes of the English 11 curriculum: students' civic engagement and participation, the development of their critical viewing and listening skills in responding to news media, and their reading comprehension and writing skills.

PART III

MEASURING MEDIA LITERACY

Chapter 6

Learning to Read the World

In September 1999, at the beginning of the second year of English 11's new incarnation as a media literacy course, teachers Elizabeth York and Joanne McGlynn invited all the presidential candidates traipsing through New Hampshire to address students on the topic of school violence. Each of the presidential candidates came to the high school auditorium and made a speech. Students in Jon Kelly's Video Production class videotaped the presentations by the presidential candidates, and many English 11 teachers saw this as a teachable moment for their focus on Media/Communication. For example, Joanne McGlynn used the opportunity to have her students examine the resulting press coverage. She set up a large poster board in one corner of her classroom with the candidates' names on top, with room for news clips underneath. Students were encouraged to bring in examples of news coverage for each of the candidates. Under Alan Keyes's and Senator Orrin Hatch's names, students had found a very small handful of news stories. But when Al Gore came to Concord High School to make a speech about school violence, the press coverage was—well, voluminous. All the rest of the space on the poster board was filled as a result of the many days of intensive national press coverage that resulted rather unexpectedly from the vice president's visit to Concord High School.

This chapter describes how Concord students learned to "read the world" through their English 11 curriculum, themselves playing a small but important part in correcting the stereotypical patterns of press coverage that were evolving in the presidential campaign in 1999. As Freire and Macedo explain in *Literacy: Reading the Word and the World* (1987), reading does not consist merely of decoding the written word or spoken language; rather, it is preceded by and intertwined with knowledge of the world and action in response to one's learning. This chapter reviews some outcomes of the impact of the English 11 curriculum on students' political efficacy and civic engagement. As I explained in Chapter 1 and the Appendix, I undertook a mixed-methods approach to study the development of students' media literacy skills. In this chapter, I report quantitative data my colleague Richard Frost and I gathered to measure students' ability to critically analyze television news and radio programming. In our study we found evidence of the impact of English 11 on students' comprehension and message analysis skills. Teacher action research shows the impact of the curriculum on students' knowledge of the 2004 presidential campaign. Together, this evidence supports the claim that media literacy education, by promoting an active, critical stance toward media messages in contemporary society, affects the development of critical thinking and civic engagement skills. As students gain the ability to comprehend news and politics by asking critical questions about media messages, they grow in knowledge and feel more empowered about their ability to understand government and politics. But they also develop skepticism about the extent to which political leaders truly represent their interests.

CRITICAL READING: THE VICE PRESIDENT GETS MISQUOTED

The national news media's coverage of Vice President Al Gore's forum at Concord High School, which took place November 30, 1999, focused not on his comments about the problem of school violence, but on a comment he made during his speech about Love Canal, the environmental disaster area in upstate New York that captured national headlines during the 1970s. According to reports in the *Washington Post* and the *New York Times,* Gore said, "I found a little place in upstate New York called Love Canal. I had the first hearing on that issue and Toone, Tenn. . . . I was the one that started it all. And it all happened because one high school student got involved."

The next day, when English 11 students read the press coverage of the event in which they had participated in, they recognized right away that something was wrong with that quote. Students asked McGlynn, "Can we see the tape?" and went back to review the videotaped footage of the event. They were even more upset when the tape confirmed that the quote was inaccurate. The students learned that Gore had not said, "I was the one that started it all." He actually had said, "That was the one that started it all," referring to a letter the young senator had received from a Tennessee high school student who had written to him about the problems with water quality and environmental health in a small rural community. The letter had led Gore to initiate the first congressional hearing on the environmental problems at Love Canal.

But in the following days, the media spin on Gore's speech took advantage of that quote from his speech at Concord High School, positioning him as (yet again) falsely taking credit for too much. In the next days, students brought in many examples of news stories about Gore's speech. One columnist pointed out that Love Canal was declared a federal disaster site 2 months before Gore—then a congressman—got involved. Students found opinion columns that said Gore's remark was his latest unjustified boast during a campaign in which he had already claimed to have invented the Internet and been the inspiration for the movie *Love Story*. The tempest in the teapot swelled as other articles appeared, each one getting pinned to McGlynn's blackboard.

One Monday morning, a student described that she had seen a commentary on a Sunday morning TV news shows, and another said that he had seen a humorous reference to the speech, described in a "Top 10 Other Achievements Claimed by Al Gore" list on David Letterman's late night show. On the television show *Hardball*, Chris Matthews jokingly compared Gore to Zelig—the colorless character in the Woody Allen film of the same name who somehow managed to turn up at momentous events. ABC's George Stephanopoulos lamented that the vice president had "revealed his Pinocchio problem."

Concord High School English 11 students were amazed and a little upset at how that one little misquote had upstaged what they felt to be the point of the forum at their high school, which was a focus on the ability of young people—as individuals—to make a difference in society. Watching and listening to Vice President Gore giving his speech in the auditorium of Concord High School, students had received a clear message about the problem of school violence and the power of individuals in their communities to make important changes that can affect large numbers of people. Because the vice president addressed the students with a directness and candor that they appreciated, the theme of personal empowerment was inspiring to many of them, young Republicans, young Democrats, and the politically apathetic alike. But all the press had emphasized was a single line from the speech—why? It seemed like the news media was seizing on a theme of "Gore as stretcher of the truth" instead of reporting on the actual content of the speech.

Students Talk Back to the Media

English 11 students tried to communicate their discovery to the media. Recalling the humorous tone of the late-night coverage of the event by David Letterman, a group of students composed and sent out a snappy news release titled "Top 10 Reasons Why Many Concord High Students Feel Betrayed by Some of the Media Coverage of Al Gore's Visit to Their School." One cold winter morning in early December, Joanne McGlynn called me, seeing her students frustrated after days of phone calls left them hoarse and exhausted. Why wouldn't journalists return the students' calls? She explained her own sense of helplessness at seeing her students ignored by the national media. McGlynn said, "They're learning the wrong lesson here. Some of them think that they're being ignored because the press has an axe to grind against Gore." I suggested that McGlynn herself call Katharine Seelye, the *New York Times* reporter who covered Gore's visit to Concord High School. Talk to her directly, I suggested. Then I called Ethan Bronner, an education editor at the *New York Times* whom I had met some years before. On the phone with him, I described the situation at Concord High School and the call I received from McGlynn. Of course, McGlynn did call reporters at the *New York Times* to complain about the coverage and, with the help of Bob Somersby of the Internet media watchdog site, *The Daily Howler,* also informed the *Washington Post* of the error. On December 7, 1999 the *Washington Post* ran a correction, in a tiny single-sentence line in the box on page 2. Three days later, the *New York Times* published a correction.

Concord students were not completely satisfied but pleased that at least the error had been recognized. They viewed the retractions in the national news as a victory of sorts. Students were learning about the importance of talking back to the often one-way news media, shifting their own perspectives from just being critics and observers of the news to becoming active participants and players. Joanne McGlynn was relieved—even though her own faith in the news media had been shaken to the foundations. She worried that her students were not learning a positive message about the role of the press in the political process.

Responding to the students' press release, the *Boston Globe* sent a reporter up to Concord to interview students and teachers, running a story on December 26 describing the students' real-world learning experience with media literacy. The students agreed it was a meaningful learning experience but also lamented their loss of innocence as readers and viewers. "How can we trust the media now?" asked junior Alyssa Spellman. "We see too much bias. We really want to know the truth. "

Finally, *U.S. News and World Report* ran an item titled "Guilty as Charged" on December 27 in which journalists admitted their part in perpetuating the error and calling the incident "a major lesson in the faults of daily journalism." Though the papers had run corrections, the journalists who reported on Gore's speech were defensive, saying the students were too focused on the one-word error and not on the big picture. "This has really been blown out of proportion," said Katharine Seelye, who covered the story for the *New York Times*. "We did get a word wrong. We corrected the word. It did not change the meaning."

In analyzing Al Gore's visit to Concord High School, Kovach and Rosenstiel (2001) write, "As journalists spend more time trying to synthesize the ever-growing stream of data pouring in through the new portals of information, the risk is they can become passive, more receivers than gatherers" (p. 76). To combat the problem they recommend this practical advice for journalists in striving to be truthful: (1) Never add anything that was not there; (2) never deceive the audience; (3) be as transparent as possible about your methods and motives; (4) rely on your own original reporting; and (5) exercise humility. Learning from a once-in-a-lifetime opportunity, English 11 students recognized the power of these same ideas and their relevance to their own growth and development as twenty-first-century communicators.

Campaign Metanarratives

Storytelling structures shape the news. In analyzing the press coverage of the presidential campaign of 2000, researchers found that press coverage of the two candidates was twice as likely to be negative toward Gore as it was toward Bush. The press was guilty of relying on "storytelling themes as a way of organizing the campaign in an engaging manner." These metanarratives provided a type of simple shorthand for understanding the candidates through stereotypical concepts like "Bush is dumb" or "Gore is a liar." Reliance on metanarrative creates problems for journalists because it trumps editorial judgment, "making it difficult for an individual reporter to write a story that differs from the popular metanarratives" (Scott & Jones, 2002, p. 22). English 11 teachers wanted their students to see how this creates problems for citizens who may not be aware of how much or what kind of information is being omitted in journalists' effort to emphasize elements of actuality that match the predefined metanarrative.

For many Concord students, the tempest over Gore's supposed ego and his tendency to stretch the truth diminished what they perceived to be the central message in his speech to them at Concord High School. Joanne McGlynn continued to be concerned that her students were becoming too cynical that fall as the political campaign heated up. She tried to correct this problem, pointing out to students that not all media coverage of the event focused on the Love Canal topic. Some media outlets, including the hometown newspaper, the Concord *Monitor*, had focused on the larger issue of school violence, which, after all, was the major theme of Gore's speech. Concord *Monitor* editor Mike Pride said that students should strive to be skeptical, not cynical. "I'm discouraged that they're disillusioned," he said. The lesson the students should take from the experience, he said, is that they "need to read a lot of sources and stay on top of things."

In 2004, students at Concord High School were still actively involved in the political process as the potential Democratic candidates came to town.

Many students who were enrolled in English 11 listened to speeches by seven of the nine Democratic candidates for president in the high school auditorium. It is a unique part of the community's political and cultural heritage and one that citizens in New Hampshire take pride in. With leadership from McGlynn, who was then serving as an assistant principal at Concord High School, students certainly got a big dose of learning how to exercise their political voice in the kind of hands-on politics that is practiced in New Hampshire.

CRITICAL VIEWING OF TELEVISION NEWS

Just how effective was the English 11 curriculum in developing students' media literacy skills, including the ability to critically analyze television news? In addressing this question in our research, we could not randomly assign students to conditions or use a comparison group within the school because all 300 plus students in Grade 11 were participating in English 11. As explained in Chapter 1, we were able to locate a control group from a different New Hampshire school district in order to implement a quasi-experimental research design that would examine differences between Concord students and a matched control group. We tested both groups of students in September 1998 and gave them the same test again the following May 1999. Readers who would like to gain additional information about the research process can find this in the Appendix, where research design, sampling, data coding, and analysis procedures are described. We published this research in *Reading Research Quarterly* (Hobbs & Frost, 2003).

To examine students' critical viewing of news and information, we provided a 5-minute news story from Channel One, originally broadcast in April of 1992, about the devastation to Miami caused by Hurricane Andrew. We selected this piece because we wanted to ensure that both the news content and the format would be unfamiliar to students (the high school does not receive Channel One). Hurricane Andrew was one of the most destructive hurricanes in the United States (before the record-breaking Hurricane Katrina hit New Orleans in 2005), with 250,000 people left homeless and $30 billion in property damage. The TV news story focused on the impact of the hurricane on the lives of South Florida teens. In the segment, news cameras took viewers to a school that was devastated by the wind and water from the hurricane and conducted interviews with young people showing how they were coping with the disaster. It also described the science of hurricanes and explained how various levels of hurricane strength are determined.

Figure 6.1. Viewing Comprehension and Analysis Activity.

Instructions: After watching the television news segment about Hurricane Andrew, answer the questions below.

Comprehension

Put the main idea of this broadcast into a sentence or two to express the main idea. Use the WHO, WHAT, WHERE, WHEN, WHY, and HOW structure to explain the story.

What was the most memorable detail? Write down one significant fact that you recall from the broadcast.

Analysis

Identify three relevant questions, facts, or information that was omitted from the message.

What was the purpose of the story (check all that apply)

_____ to inform   _____ to entertain   _____ to persuade

_____ for self expression   _____ to make money   _____ to teach

List the techniques that were used to attract and hold viewers' attention.

What values or points of view were represented in the message?

List three ways that this news story was similar to and different from local or national television news.

| *Similarities* | *Differences* |
| Between this news story and regular news | Between this news story and regular news |

Who is the target audience for this message? (Place a check mark in the appropriate categories below)

_____ men   _____ Whites
_____ women   _____ African Americans
                                   _____ Asian Americans
_____ 2–11-year-olds   _____ Hispanics
_____ 12–17-year-olds   _____ Other
_____ 18–25-year-olds
_____ 25–40-year-olds   _____ poor people
_____ 40–60-year-olds   _____ working-class people
_____ 60 and up   _____ middle-class people
                                   _____ upper-middle-class people
                                   _____ wealthy people

Give reasons explaining why you made your choices.

Figure 6.1 shows the instrument we used to measure viewing comprehension and analysis. It was adapted from research conducted previously in another high school to measure media literacy skills of ninth graders (Hobbs & Frost, 1999). The measures that appear on this instrument are discussed in the following sections of this chapter.

VIEWING COMPREHENSION

To assess viewing comprehension, we used two measures. In the first question, students were asked to summarize the main idea of the newsmagazine TV news story. In responding, students were asked to identify the "who, what, where, when, why, and how" by writing sentences to capture the main ideas of the story. Students' answers were scored on a scale ranging from 0 to 3 points. A student who wrote: "People in South Florida were forced to evacuate their homes after the hurricane hit in 1992 and many teens were worried about their schools and families because a level five hurricane is so destructive" received three points. A student who wrote: "The hurricane was scary" received no points. We found statistically significant differences between performance in the control group and the treatment group. Students' ability to identify main ideas after watching a television newscast improved, and we found statistically significant differences when comparing the control group's mean of 2.25 to the treatment group mean of 2.85. (Throughout the book, I include only those findings that were found to be statistically significant, meaning that the differences between the groups were unlikely to have occurred by chance.) Students who had taken English 11 were more effective in summarizing the main ideas of a television news broadcast than those in the control group.

Another measure of viewing comprehension, the second question in the instrument, asked students to describe a specific informational detail they recalled from the broadcast. Students received points based on the level of specificity of the detail. For example a student who wrote, "Fifteen people have been killed" received 3 points, while a student who wrote, "The storm did a lot of damage" received 1 point. Other specific details described by the students were factors that contributed to the cost of the storm damage, the wind speed category designation system, and the part of the hurricane that is most damaging to the coastal areas. No statistically significant differences were found in comparing the scores of students in the control group to those in the treatment group. English 11 students at Concord High School were better able to recall and summarize the main ideas of an informational news broadcast, but their ability to recall specific details showed no differences between groups.

Table 6.1. Media Literacy Skills in Responding to TV News and Radio News.

Variable	Control n = 89	Treatment n = 287
Critical Viewing of News		
Identify message purpose as "to entertain"	18%	33%**
Identify the purpose as "to make money"	16%	23%*
Identify creative construction techniques	1.40	2.20***
Identify point of view	1.79	1.93***
Identify omitted information	1.54	2.01***
Identify similarities between stimulus and other TV news	1.99	2.23***
Identify differences between stimulus and other TV news	1.75	2.12***
Critical Listening Skills		
Identify message purpose as "to persuade"	29%	56%**
Identify creative construction techniques	.63	1.28***
Identify omitted information	1.89	1.88

*p<.05
**p<.01
*** p<.001

Measuring Critical Viewing of News

Compared to the control group, Grade 11 students at Concord High School were much better able to demonstrate critical viewing skills of recognizing the (1) purpose, (2) creative construction techniques, (3) point of view, (4) omissions found in television news, and (5) making an effective comparison–contrast.

First, we asked, could students identify the *purpose* of the media message? After viewing the short news story on Hurricane Andrew, students were asked to identify the purpose of the media message, and they were offered six choices: to inform, to persuade, to entertain, to make money, for self-expression, and to teach. They could check as many as they thought applied. As shown in Table 6.1, English 11 students in the treatment group were considerably more likely to identify the purpose as "to entertain." While only 18% of the control group recognized this as one of the purposes of the broadcast, 33% of the treatment group recognized this, a statistically significant difference between groups. There were small but statistically significant differences between groups in the ability to recognize the purpose of the broadcast as "to make money," with only 16% of the control group identifying this purpose as compared with 23% of the treatment group. Students at Concord High School were more able than the control group to recognize the blurring of information, entertainment, and marketing in television news.

Could students recognize the *creative construction techniques* used in television news? Students were asked to list the attention-getting rhetorical and creative production techniques, and we coded these on a scale from 0 to 3 points. A student received 3 points for this answer: "The music and the flashing pictures in the beginning of the broadcast kept your attention. Watching different shots of the hurricane and how some people reacted also captured my attention." A student who wrote, "The upbeat music was dramatic and powerful" received 1 point. A student who wrote, "Shock" received no points. Media literacy students in the treatment group had higher scores than students in the control group in the ability to identify attention-getting message construction techniques. Control group students had a mean score of 1.40 as compared with the treatment group's mean score of 2.20, a statistically significant finding. English 11 students were able to recognize and describe the use of teen anchors, dramatic music, emotional interviews, intense footage of wind and rain from the hurricane, interviews with teens, and editing montage as strategies used by the news to attract and hold audience attention.

Could students recognize the *point of view* presented in the broadcast? Students were asked to identify the point of view of the television segment they viewed, and we coded their answers on a scale from 0 to 3 points. After reading a large sample of student responses, we created a list of statements representing the various points of view that students identified, and we assigned point values reflecting their quality. A student who wrote: "Much of the story was given from the point of view of young people who were affected by the storm" received three points. A student who wrote, "Hurricanes are destructive, dangerous, and unpredictable" received only one point. While both the control group and the Concord English 11 students improved from pretest to posttest, analysis revealed small but statistically significant differences between the two groups on the ability to identify point of view. Control group students scored an average of 1.79 on the point of view measure as compared to 1.93 for Concord English 11 students.

Could students generate ideas about the *omitted information* of a broadcast? Recognizing omissions is a skill that calls upon active processing of information and the ability to synthesize relationships between ideas. Recognizing omissions has been seen as a vital dimension for identifying the point of view in an informational text (Kovach & Rosenstiel, 2001). This question also measures a dimension of strategic, higher order comprehension because in identifying omitted information, students must be able to generate new information connected to a topic. Concord students were better able to generate a number of statements, questions, and ideas that were omitted from the television news broadcast about hurricanes. We asked students to develop a list of ideas or information that was left out of the media message or to write down unanswered questions that lingered in their minds. Comparing treatment group to control group, there were statistically significant differences in the ability to identify omitted information, comparing the control group mean of 1.54 to the treatment group mean of 2.01. In the course of participating in English 11, Concord students were repeatedly invited to reflect on how a reader could detect the bias and/or the point of view of a media message by learning to notice omissions. The data show that, when compared to the matched control group, students in the media literacy program were better able to identify information that was omitted—by imagining unanswered questions and thinking about specific facts or other points of view that were not presented in the broadcast.

Could students *compare and contrast* the teen-focused news program with the TV news formats used on local and national news? Comparison-contrast is a fundamental strategy used to promote critical thinking. Students were asked to "List three ways that this news story was similar to and different from local or national TV news." Students who were more familiar with the formats of local and national television news would be expected to answer this question with ease. Space was provided to list similarities separately from differences and responses were coded on a three-point scale. In responding to this question, students identified similarities including the following: the use of interviews, maps and graphs, anchor people addressing the viewer directly, taped footage from on location, voice-overs explaining visuals, rapid editing, and dramatic statistics. For identifying similarities, mean scores for the control group of 1.99 were compared with the treatment group mean of 2.23, and there was a statistically significant difference between groups.

Students described differences between this Channel One broadcast and local and national TV views by noticing elements like the use of dramatic music, the wider variety of racial and ethnic groups depicted, the use of teenagers as anchors, the large number of teens interviewed as sources on camera, the use of information graphics, and the level of background detail provided. For identifying differences, students in the control group averaged 1.75 items as compared to the English 11 treatment group mean of 2.12 items, a statistically significant difference between groups. Students taking English 11 at Concord High School recognized that the Channel One broadcast fit clearly within the genre of television news but was specifically created to appeal to the target audience of 12–17-year-olds. As a result, students recognized some of the unique production qualities of the broadcast that provided more background information about the news event and used youth-oriented techniques designed to provoke viewers' emotional response. English 11 students had frequent and regular opportunities to analyze television news and current events and their increased familiarity with these texts may have increased their ability to use comparison–contrast as an analytic tool.

CRITICAL LISTENING SKILLS

Listening skills are certainly the bastard stepchild of English language arts. While listening is the first language mode that children acquire, many teachers often assume that listening skills develop naturally and do not require instruction. No widely accepted model for teaching listening skills has developed (Hyslop & Tone, 1988), even though the topic is addressed in significant ways by scholars and practitioners in medicine, nursing, public health, education, language learning, clinical psychology, and communication. Listening researchers themselves use a wide variety of constructs to capture the complex elements of the cognitive and affective processes of listening. Attention, memory, empathy, interpretation, emotional response, characteristics of the stimuli, and context all affect the listening process (Witkin & Trochim, 1997).

Because listening plays a major lifelong role in the processes of learning and communication, some English language arts teachers in the K–12 grades have attempted to strengthen listening skills using instructional models from studies of reading comprehension (Field, 1988). For example, listening comprehension skills can be strengthened when (1) initial discussion activates prior knowledge and ties new concepts to students' backgrounds and life experiences; (2) a goal or purpose for listening is explicitly identified; (3) representational maps, note taking, or other activity is used during listening to help focus attention and reinforce concepts; and (4) response questions promote literal, interpretive, and critical responses (Hyslop & Tone, 1988).

My colleague Richard Frost and I wondered if the English 11 curriculum would strengthen students' listening to radio news and commentary. We adapted the viewing comprehension and analysis measure described earlier for use with an audio stimulus: a short broadcast from a 1998 episode of *All*

Things Considered. This National Public Radio (NPR) show included a 3-minute radio commentary about David Brinkley, a well-respected television news personality who had just become a spokesman for an agribusiness multinational corporation, Archer Daniels Midland, "the Supermarket to the World." The broadcast used a combination of first-person narrative, interview clips, audio segments from television programs, and music; it described the tendency for distinguished athletes, journalists, and celebrities to "sell out" on behalf of corporate America. The author bemoaned the blurring of marketing and information that has become a way of life for American celebrities and urged Brinkley to be true to the ideals of American journalism and give up his work as a shill for corporate America. After listening to the radio commentary, questions asked students to identify the main ideas and supporting facts of the broadcast. Critical listening skills were also measured by asking students to identify the purpose, target audience, and point of view of the article, to describe what attention-getting techniques were used, and to identify three pieces of information that were missing from the article.

To assess listening comprehension, we used two measures, identical in structure to the approach used to measure viewing comprehension. First students were asked to summarize the main idea of the radio commentary. In responding, students were asked to identify the "who, what, where, when, why, and how" by writing sentences to capture the main ideas of the story. Both groups improved from pretest to posttest, but control group students' mean score of 2.31 was lower than English 11 students, who had a mean score of 2.49, a small but statistically significant difference. Students were also asked to describe a specific informational detail of the broadcast, but as with measures of news viewing, we found no statistically significant differences on this variable between groups.

Could students recognize the purpose of the audio commentary? Students were asked to select from the following purposes, checking as many as applied: to inform, to entertain, to make money, to persuade, to teach, and for self-expression. As shown in Table 6.1, only 29% of control group students identified the message's purpose as persuasive compared with 56% of English 11 students who made this identification, a statistically significant difference. This media message was very obviously a persuasive radio commentary, with a clear tone, voice, and point of view. Concord English 11 students also recognized that this radio commentary was expressing the point of view of a particular individual. Only 30% of control group students identified the message as self-expressive at the posttest as compared with 60% of English 11 students. Compared to the control group, students enrolled in English 11 were more likely to see the broadcast as persuasive and created for purposes of self-expression.

Could English 11 students identify the creative construction techniques of the radio commentary? We asked students to list the techniques they noticed while listening, and we awarded 0 to 3 points based on their responses. Control group students identified a mean of only .63 techniques at posttest as compared with English 11 students, who identified a mean of 1.28 techniques. Students described techniques they noticed in the short broadcast, including the use of music, multiple interviews, sound samples from television news and advertising, naming celebrities and athletes, and asking rhetorical questions. The ability to recognize such techniques demonstrates an understanding that all media messages are constructed.

Could students recognize the point of view of the radio news broadcast? The piece from *All Things Considered*, introduced by Bob Edwards and performed by Rem Ryder, was an opinion commentary. We scored students' answers on a 3-point scale and awarded points based on the completeness of student response. For example, a student who wrote, "This guy thinks that Brinkley has hurt the public by moving from news anchor to corporate spokesperson for a big business" would receive 3 points. A student received 1 point for the response, "Journalists are mad." Control group students identified a mean of 1.37 techniques at posttest as compared with English 11 students, who identified a mean of 1.50 techniques. There were statistically significant differences between English 11 students and the control group in the ability to identify the point of view that was depicted in the radio news commentary. Recognizing point of view is a key dimension of media literacy.

Could students generate questions, statements, ideas, or other information that was omitted from the radio commentary? We asked students to develop a list of ideas or information that was left out of the media message or to write down unanswered questions that lingered in their minds. No statistically significant differences were found between control group students ($M = 1.89$) and those in English 11 ($M = 1.88$) on this measure.

Listening is an active literacy process requiring the skills of attending, predicting, hypothesizing, checking, revising, and generalizing in order to make meaning from spoken language. With iPods, MP3 players, and podcasts now a ubiquitous feature of the adolescent's cultural environment, English language arts teachers should continue to explore the ways that students' critical listening skills can be developed through media literacy activities.

STUDENTS' POLITICAL EFFICACY

In surveying students at the beginning of the 1998 school year and again at the end of the school year in the late spring of 1999, we only included a few questionnaire items that provided some insight on changes in students' sense of political efficacy. The modest evidence I share below about the impact of the program on students' political attitudes is present as preliminary evidence about a complex phenomenon. At the time my colleague Richard Frost and I constructed the questionnaire, we did not fully appreciate how much the news, politics, and current events would become part of the classroom curriculum of English 11; as a result, we did not include a comprehensive measurement of students' political attitudes or civic engagement. Still, we did find some intriguing patterns in the data that provide evidence that media literacy education may affect the development of a sense of political efficacy.

Political efficacy is defined as citizens' faith and trust in government and their own belief that they can understand and influence political affairs (Wolbrecht & Campbell, 2005). It is commonly measured by surveys and used as an indicator for the broader health of civil society. Feelings of efficacy are highly correlated with participation in social and political life, especially voting. Parents and schools play an important role in shaping the attitudes of children and adolescents that contribute to later voting and other forms of civic engagement. Researchers have found that the content of the curriculum, high educational expectations, and a classroom climate in which students are encouraged to actively participate by expressing their opinions are important factors in building a sense of political efficacy. Watching television news, reading newspapers, and discussing politics with parents are also ways to enhance both the knowledge of civic matters and the inclination to vote (Torney-Purta, 2004).

We measured political efficacy by asking students to respond to three statements:

1. Sometimes politics and government seem so complicated that a person like me can't really understand what's going on.
2. I don't think that public officials care much about what people like me think.
3. Over the years, government leaders pay a good deal of attention to what the people think when they decide what to do.

Students at both Concord High School and at the control school were asked to signal their level of agreement or disagreement on a 5-point scale ranging from "strongly agree" to "strongly disagree." The first two questions are composed as negative statements, so that a higher score on these items indicates a more negative attitude.

Table 6.2. Pretest and Posttest Measures of Political Efficacy by Gender, Concord High School.

Statement	*Gender*	*Pretest* $n = 287$	*Posttest* $n = 287$
Sometimes politics and government seem so complicated that a person like me can't really understand what's going on.	GIRLS	3.32	3.14 ***
	BOYS	2.76	2.82
I don't think that public officials care much about what people like me think.	GIRLS	3.27	3.29
	BOYS	2.91	3.07 *
Over the years, government leaders pay a good deal of attention to what the people think when they decide what to do.	GIRLS	2.94	2.69 **
	BOYS	3.10	3.01

*p<.05
**p<.01
***p<.001

Gender Differences

Gender differences in political behavior have been found in many different countries—women are less politically active than men and have a weaker sense of political efficacy (Wolbrecht & Campbell, 2005). Researchers suspect that socialization factors contribute to such gender differences. Girls may learn to express less interest in political activity because of observed political gender roles—how many female politicians are they exposed to? Or it may be that girls are influenced by the political behavior they see in their own homes—who reads the newspaper and participates in talk about politics? Other arguments have been made about the content of civic education in schools and the agenda of current political debates.

Comparing Concord High School students as they answered the questions above, first in September and again the following May, we found statistically significant differences between girls and boys in responding to these questions. Table 6.2 shows that girls and boys began Grade 11 with different levels of political efficacy in terms of their perceptions of the complexity of politics and government. At the beginning of the school year, girls had stronger feelings of being unable to understand politics (pretest M = 3.32 for girls, pretest M = 2.76 for boys). By the end of the 1998–99 school year, girls' level of agreement that politics and government were too complex to understand had declined (posttest M = 3.14 for girls, posttest M = 2.82 for boys). This was a statistically significant change in the girls' attitude about the complexity of politics that was unlikely to have occurred by chance. At the end of their 11th-grade year, young women at Concord High School were more confident that they could understand the complexities of politics and government. The gap between the attitudes of females and males in terms of their sense of their own political engagement had diminished, but was not completely eliminated. Young women students became empowered during the school year in terms of their own ability to make sense of government and politics.

But girls also developed more skepticism about the political leadership as compared with boys. For example, students responded to the statement, "Over the years, government leaders pay a good deal of attention to what the people think then they decide what to do." Table 6.2 shows some differences evident at the time of the pretest between girls and boys. Boys were more optimistic about government leaders paying attention to the public, giving a higher level of agreement with this statement than girls (pretest M = 2.94 for girls, pretest M = 3.10 for boys). At the end of the school years, girls' level of agreement with this statement dropped from 2.94 to 2.69, while for boys, the drop was less precipitous.

Students grew in skepticism as they became more knowledgeable and gained a sense of political empowerment. Media literacy instruction may have played a role in increasing both adolescents' skepticism and their sense of efficacy about the comprehensibility of politics and government. But because this research did not develop a theoretical model for examining the impact of media literacy on political attitudes and behaviors, this evidence is limited and preliminary. The quasi-experimental research design limits claims about causality. Students were not randomly assigned to the media literacy program of instruction since the program was required for all Grade 11 students, and even though the control group school was closely matched on a number of demographic characteristics, there may be unmeasured differences between the groups that could have accounted for the findings we obtained. Future research should be conducted to explore the relationship between media literacy and the development of behaviors and attitudes that contribute to citizenship.

THE ADOLESCENT AS CITIZEN

In 2003, English 11 teacher Denise Fournier surveyed her students' knowledge of the political process, their news media use, and their perception of media bias as part of an action research project. *Teacher action research* is an evaluation method designed to engage educational practitioners in the assessment and improvement of their own practice. It can be an individual tool, helping classroom teachers to reconsider their teaching methods or to adapt in order to solve a problem. It can also be a community activity, helping teams of educators to assess problems in schools, enact changes, and reassess. Although teacher action research looks different in every context, it is, in general, (1) a nontraditional and community-based form of educational evaluation; (2) carried out by educators, not outside researchers or evaluators; (3) focused on improving teaching and learning, but also on social and environmental factors that affect the nature and success of teaching and learning; (4) formative, not summative—an ongoing process of evaluation, recommendation, practice, reflection, and reevaluation; and (5) change-oriented, and undertaken with the assumption that change is needed in a given context (Gorski, 2004).

Fournier asked her English 11 students to complete a questionnaire during the first week of school in the fall of 2003 and again in late January 2004 when the New Hampshire primary had ended. Table 6.3 shows that students increased their familiarity with the politicians running for president and gained awareness of how to get political information. Their overall perceptions of the honesty of politicians did not change much. Students increased the frequency of their TV news viewing, with 19% watching every day at the beginning of the school year and 36% viewing every day by the middle of the school year. Their newspaper reading also increased in frequency, with only 21% of students reporting that they read a newspaper daily at the time of the pretest and 41% reporting daily newspaper reading at the posttest. Online newspaper reading increased too. Pretest results showed that 38% of Fournier's English 11 students claimed that they never read online newspapers at the beginning of the school year, but 5 months later, 89% of students reported that they looked at online newspapers once a week or more often. For adolescents, this is a dramatic change in media consumption behavior. Perhaps students were engaging in teacher-pleasing, or perhaps students became genuinely more interested in news and current events.

Teens at Concord High School were simultaneously inspired by their experience with media literacy education to feel more empowered to understand politics; at the same time, they became more skeptical about the actions of politicians and the news media in relation to their own interests and needs as citizens. Girls especially were more likely to see politicians as engaged in work that did not represent their interests as citizens. And yet despite these attitudes, the young women and young men of Concord High

Table 6.3. Informal Measures of Students' Civic Engagement.

	Pretest $n = 41$	Posttest $n = 39$
How many of the 10 candidates running for president in 2004 can you name?	1.8	9.0
On a scale of 5 to 1, how honest do you think candidates are who are running for president?	3.04	2.92
How many newspapers can you name?	3.3	6.0
How many cable news networks can you name?	1.4	2.1
How often do you watch the news?		
Every day	19%	36%
Two–three times a week	26%	33%
Once a week	33%	26%
Never	21%	5%
How often do you read a newspaper?		
Every day	21%	41%
Two–three times a week	33%	26%
Once a week	28%	28%
Never	16%	5%
How often do you read news on the Internet?		
Every day	9%	12%
Two–three times a week	21%	26%
Once a week	31%	51%
Never	38%	11%

Note. Data collected by Denise Fournier. May not add to 100% due to rounding error.

School were increasingly engaged in discussion about government and politics by actively participating in it—finding ways to enter into the debate and have their voices heard.

Researchers know that young people develop political concepts in their childhood through their everyday experiences of familiar institutions such as the school and the family. Notions of authority, fairness and justice, rules and laws, power and control are all formed long before young people can express their views in the form of voting (Buckingham, 1999). In sorting out how journalistic metanarratives about presidential campaigns conflicted with students' own interpretations of a politician's speech, it is clear that teenagers at Concord High School possessed some of the intellectual and critical abilities that are components of political maturity. They participated in talking back to the media and reflected on the role of the press in shaping contemporary political discourse. They benefited from opportunities to "read the word and the world" through systematic opportunities for learning that connected literacy to life.

Chapter 7

Measuring Advertising Analysis Skills

In many classrooms in the United States, Great Britain, Canada, and Australia, advertising is a topic of inquiry, and print and TV ads are used in classrooms as "texts" to be studied. As discussed in Chapter 4, advertising has been studied in high school since the early 1950s, when post–World War II educators recognized the need to introduce the concepts of propaganda and public opinion. Drawing upon a tradition underway in the United Kingdom, Canada, and Australia for the past 25 years, the study of advertising and persuasion are now routinely included in English language arts in the United States (Brown, 2005). In many classrooms, students are invited to analyze, learn about, design, and create advertising in print, visual, video, and multimedia formats as part of their instruction. For example, in 1998 the state of Texas added "viewing and representing skills" alongside "reading, writing, speaking, and listening skills" for students in Grades 4 through 12, and state curriculum frameworks make explicit reference to the genres of advertising, documentary, film drama, and news. The ability to analyze advertising was recently included as a component of the high-stakes TAAS test for 10th graders in Texas, involving students' ability to identify the persuasive techniques used in a specific print ad. The state of New Hampshire has also used similar questions in their statewide tests for Grade 10 students.

The Concord High School English 11 teachers believed that their instructional lessons on advertising, persuasion, and propaganda were some of the most effective and powerful components of their curriculum. But what impact did the instruction have on students' ability to critically analyze advertising? What did students actually learn about advertising? How did the learning experience affect students' attitudes about advertising and consumer culture? This chapter describes the quantitative evidence my colleague Robert Frost and I found to better understand the impact of the English 11 curriculum on students' knowledge and analysis skills. As explained in Chapter 1 and the Appendix, we gathered data from English 11 students at Concord High School and a matched control group during the 1998–99 school year. Students were tested in September at the beginning of the school year and again the following May. We report changes in students' knowledge of the advertising production process as well as their ability to critically analyze a specific advertising message. We were particularly interested in examining students' recognition of the target audience, purpose, point of view, and creative construction techniques.

What is the impact of teaching about advertising on students? There is evidence that shows that learning about advertising and discussions about advertising in school can reduce children's vulnerability to advertising appeals and increase their ability to produce counterarguments in response to advertising. For example, Christenson (1992) developed a 3-minute video about advertising and showed it to children ages 6 to 12, finding that children who viewed the video were more aware of commercials and expressed less trust in commercials in general. In another study, short films were made to show children how television ads use various techniques to persuade. The researchers found that the children who watched the most TV were initially most susceptible to commercial influence but they were also the most influenced by the educational films about advertising (Roberts, Christenson, Gibson, Mooser, & Goldberg, 1980). Under some conditions, learning about advertising seems to promote critical thinking in responding to media messages.

One measure used to evaluate students' media literacy skills in responding to advertising is the *counterargument*. In cognitive information-processing theory, thoughts in response to persuasive communication may trigger an attitude change. When people are exposed to persuasion, they relate it to preexisting thoughts that they already have about the product, service, images, or narrative depicted. The way the recipient of the communication manipulates, elaborates, and integrates the information affects the persuasiveness of the message (Potter, 2004). Of course, people are more likely to be persuaded by messages about which they have previously thought optimistically—and they're less likely to be persuaded if they had generated negative thoughts about the product. Counterarguments are usually defined as negative thoughts about a product. Researchers found that teens who had discussed alcohol advertising in school were able to provide nearly twice as many counterarguments in response to alcohol advertising after viewing a 20-minute sports or comedy program with ads including four beer advertisements as compared with students who did not receive any opportunities to discuss alcohol advertising in school (Slater et al., 1996).

COGNITIVE DEFENSES FOR RESISTING ADVERTISING

Thirty years ago, the concept of *cognitive defenses* was developed: an idea that youth can become capable of resisting advertising appeals by perceiving the purpose behind the message and understanding how persuasive techniques work (Rossiter & Robertson, 1974). Developmental psychologists have suggested that, for children, understanding the selling intent of ads requires five component skills: (1) the ability to distinguish program from commercial; (2) recognizing that an ad was created by an author or external source; (3) appreciating that an ad is designed to reach an intended target audience; (4) identifying the symbolic and constructed nature of advertising; and (5) being able to generate real-world examples of a product not meeting the expectations generated by the advertising. Researchers have examined children's ability to identify the purpose of advertising, finding that by age 10 or 11, children are able to identify the persuasive intent of advertising, with younger children seeing commercials as largely informative (see Young, 1990, for review of research). In responding to food advertising in particular, children did not generally activate critical thinking skills or generate counterarguments in responding to appeals for cereal, candy, and soft drinks (Ross, Campbell, Huston-Stein, & Wright, 1981).

But every kid has learned from life experience that the product as advertised is not the product as purchased. Media literacy skills may first be activated in young children through the inevitable discovery that the "zoom-zoom" noise in the toy commercial, with its animated special effects and zippy production values, is not the same noise the toy makes when you roll it on the kitchen floor in your home. What does it take to activate children's skepticism about advertising? Fourth graders responded to advertising using an open-ended cognitive response measurement in which respondents view or read a media message and then list the thoughts and feelings that they recall arising during the processing of the message, sometimes in response to one or more probes to cue children's response. Researchers found a relationship between knowledge about advertising and children's ability to generate skeptical and critical ideas in response to direct questions about advertising. However, when they examined students' noncued responses to advertising, they found that children did not generate critical thoughts during ad exposure (Brucks, Armstrong, & Goldberg, 1988). This evidence suggests that even though children may have skeptical attitudes about advertising, unless they are cued to respond cognitively to an ad, they may not activate this knowledge in responding to a message.

While older children and teens may have more knowledge about advertising, they also may not necessarily activate critical thinking skills in response to advertising or have more skepticism about advertising in general. Boush, Friestad, and Rose (1994) measured middle school students' knowledge of advertiser tactics and effects, and their skepticism of advertising. Tactics included the use of celebrities, music, humor, cartoons, product comparisons, product demonstrations, and depictions of target audience. They found increased knowledge about advertiser tactics over a 9-month period, but no overall increase in advertising skepticism. They did find an association between knowledge about advertising tactics and being more skeptical of advertising:

> Improving students' understanding of the way advertising works may have more potential for creating discerning consumers than has changing students' general attitudes. . . . Exhortations to "not believe everything you see on TV" are, therefore, less likely to produce changes in the processing of advertising claims than is a more careful analysis of advertisements that lays bare the persuasive device. (p. 172)

In reviewing and evaluating the literature on advertising and children, Young (1990) criticized the validity of research that has used superficial measures of children's skepticism including responses to attitude statements using Likert-type scales. Even young children are aware of the social desirability of attitudes opposing advertising, he claims. Instead, Young argues that knowledge about the tactics used by advertisers to persuade and skills like being able to understand the purpose and function of a media message are key components needed to acquire critical thinking skills about advertising.

KNOWLEDGE OF THE ADVERTISING PRODUCTION PROCESS

Knowledge about media institutions, processes, and effects is a vital element of learning to be media literate. Potter (2004) states that five knowledge structures underlie media literacy: knowledge of media content, media industries, and media effects, and real-world information, and knowledge of the self. He wrote, "With knowledge in these five areas, people are much more aware during the information-processing tasks and are, therefore, more able to make better decisions about seeking out information, working with that information, and constructing meaning from it that will be useful to serve their own goals" (p. 69). Potter doesn't explicitly acknowledge the value of learning about media production processes, emphasizing instead knowledge about media industries, economics, ownership and control, and marketing.

Other scholars insist that understanding creative composition and production skills are essential components of media literacy (Bruce, in press; Buckingham, Grahame, & Sefton-Green, 1995). According to this argument, when students experience the processes of brainstorming, researching the target audiences, developing a purpose, and composing and designing a message, they build knowledge and ways of problem solving that in turn directly shape analytic skills. This is somewhat analogous to the longstanding arguments among literacy educators who recognize the inseparable relationship between reading and writing (Hansen, 2003). In addition, when students construct work for a "real" audience, it builds cooperative communication skills that "redefine the conventional hierarchies of learning . . . through the genuinely democratic process of constructing meanings from and for the community" (Grahame, 1991, p. 168).

My colleague Richard Frost and I wanted to measure students' knowledge of the media production process. In the fall of 1998 and again in 1999, we showed students a 30-second commercial twice and asked them to write down all the steps that were taken in the process of constructing the ad. The commercial we selected was the humorous and relatively famous "Cindy Crawford drinks Pepsi" ad which features two boys watching Cindy stop at a rural western truck stop, get out of her bright red sportscar, put quarters in the Pepsi machine, and chug down a Diet Pepsi with gusto. After showing the ad twice, we gave students a sheet that asked them to think about all the steps involved in the creation of the ad. Students were then asked to list up to 15 steps in the production process. We coded their statements against a list of preproduction, production, and postproduction processes that we had developed based on a description of the advertising production process as identified by a number of authors and industry experts (Adams, 1977; Pungente & Marcuse, 1997; Schudson, 1984; Schwartz, 1973).

We found that English 11 students had learned a lot about the complex process of creating an ad campaign. Compared to students in the control group, evidence from this study demonstrated statistically significant gains in learning about both the preproduction and postproduction processes among English 11 students. Table 7.1 shows that students in the media literacy treatment group were more likely to describe the need for producers to identify a specific target audience, comparing the control group posttest mean score of only 3% to the media literacy treatment posttest mean score of 12%. Students enrolled in English 11 were more likely to describe the need for producers to brainstorm ideas and engage in planning, comparing the control group mean score of only 31% to the media literacy treatment mean score of 70%. There were statistically significant differences between the control group and students in English 11 in recognizing that an idea for an ad campaign must be approved by the company before going into production. Only 3% of control group students made this identification as compared with 24% of English 11 students. Students in the media literacy treatment group were also more likely to describe the need for producers to plan the visuals by creating a storyboard, comparing the control group mean score of 7% to the media literacy treatment

Table 7.1. Student Knowledge of the Advertising Production Process.

	Control Group *n = 89*	*Treatment Group* *n = 287*
Preproduction		
Identification of target audience	3%	12%*
Planning and brainstorming	31%	70%***
Idea is approved by company	3%	24%***
Write a script	51%	48%
Plan the visuals	7%	16%**
Hire talent to appear in the ad	88%	89%
Select location and props	72%	63%
Create or select the music	24%	13%*
Production		
Rehearse with talent	54%	47%
Film the ad	81%	81%
Postproduction		
Edit the images	82%	83%
Add the music	23%	22%
Add the graphic text on screen	3%	1%
Get final approval from company	15%	23%**
Buy airtime from networks	21%	24%
Broadcast the ad	5%	7%
Measure impact on sales	3%	19%***

Note. Data are expressed in percentages.

*p<.05

**p<.01

*** p<.001

group mean score of 16%. However, control group students were more likely to monitor music than English 11 students.

In examining students' understanding of the postproduction process, there were statistically significant differences between the control group and the English 11 students in the ability to recognize that the final ad required approval from the company. Only 15% of control group students included this item as compared with 23% of students in the media literacy treatment. Concord students were also far more likely to recognize the producers' attempt to measure the impact of the ad by looking at changes in sales volume. While 1% of control group students identified this, 19% of media literacy students included this idea in their list. This evidence shows that English 11 students had acquired a deeper understanding of many of the economic dimensions of advertising.

SKILLS FOR ANALYZING ADVERTISING

Teachers wondered whether their lessons, readings, and activities on advertising had an impact on helping students in Concord High School acquire critical thinking skills in responding to advertising, particularly for products related to adolescent health. To measure media literacy skills in responding to advertising, students received the black-and-white copy of a print alcohol ad for Miller Beer, shown in Figure 7.1. The ad, originally produced for Miller Beer, was included in the *AdSmarts* media literacy curriculum (Watson et al., 1992). The ad features two young African American men dressed in suits. The phrase, "Life in the Cold Lane" is prominent, and the lower right hand corner of the ad contains a small logo featuring a traffic yield sign with the words "Miller Brewing Company reminds you to please Think When You Drink."

Students were asked to complete a series of paper-and-pencil response questions while viewing the ad. As described in the Appendix, students' media literacy skills were measured using both open-ended and checklist items to determine students' ability to identify purpose, target audience, construction techniques, and message subtext. Figure 7.2 displays the questionnaire. We created media literacy measures to assess students' ability to identify (1) the assumed target audience; (2) the specific techniques employed in the construction of the ad, including visual and verbal elements, symbolism, and graphic design; (3) the assumed message subtext or unstated message of the ad; and (4) the ad's assumed purpose. This approach was based on the work of Australian researchers who had developed a measure of students' media literacy skills that included paper-and-pencil tests of students' ability to analyze a print ad (Quin & MacMahon, 1995), and there is some correspondence with the measures of cognitive defenses as described by Rossiter and Robertson (1974). Although the readers of a media message rarely have knowledge of the creator's actual target audience, subtext, or purpose in designing a message, critical readers may make inferences about these dimensions of a media message using clues in the message text and images along with their knowledge of media industries (Messaris, 1994). We measured these media literacy skills using the procedures described below.

Who Is the Target Audience?

To measure students' assessment of target audience, students were given a checklist of six different age-range categories (from age 2 to over age 55);

Figure 7.1. Ad Stimulus.

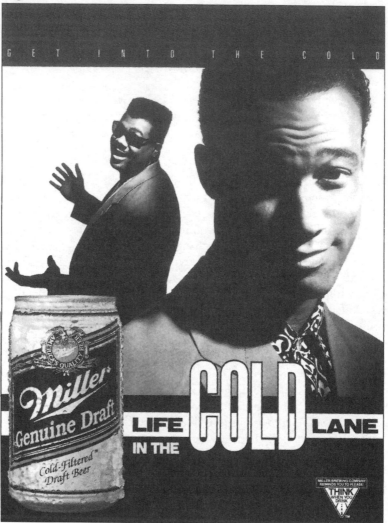

two genders; five different racial categories; five different social-class categories (from "poor people" to "wealthy"). They were asked, "Who is the target audience for this message?" and invited to check all that apply. Concord teachers who responded to these test items agreed that the categories of race, age, gender, and social class were the most relevant variables in relation to this ad.

Students were expected to provide a rationale for their choices of target audience. An open-ended question asked students to provide a description of

Figure 7.2. Advertising Analysis Activity.

Instructions: Look at the ad [provided in Figure 7.1] as you answer these questions.

Who is the target audience for this message? (Place a check mark in the appropriate categories below)

_____ men	_____ Whites
_____ women	_____ African Americans
	_____ Asian Americans
_____ 2 – 7 year olds	_____ Hispanics
_____ 8 – 12 year olds	_____ Other
_____ 13 – 17 year olds	
_____ 18 – 21 year olds	_____ poor people
_____ 22 – 25 year olds	_____ working-class people
_____ 25 – 35 year olds	_____ middle-class people
_____ 35 – 45 year olds	_____ upper-middle-class people
_____ 45 – 55 year olds	_____ wealthy people
_____ 55 and up	

What visual information in the ad supports your answer?

List the techniques that were used to attract and hold viewers' attention.

What is the purpose of the message?

What is the subtext of the message? What values are embedded in this message?

What does the small logo in the right-hand corner mean?

Table 7.2. Ability to Identify the Target Audience for an Ad.

	Control Group *n = 89*	*Treatment Group* *n = 287*
Age		
2–11	2%	1%
12–17	22%	28%
18–25	92%	94%
25–40	79%	79%
40–60	33%	24%*
60+	42%	10%***
Gender		
Male	96%	98%
Female	45%	33%**
Race		
White	60%	49%***
African American	96%	98%
Hispanic	57%	35%***
Asian	44%	25%***
Other	57%	35%***
Class		
Poor	43%	24%***
Working class	40%	47%
Middle class	93%	91%
Upper-middle class	49%	48%
Wealthy	38%	29%
Identification of visual or verbal evidence to support answer	1.63	2.24***

*p<.05
**p<.01
*** p<.001

specific visual information from the ad that they used to support their answers. These responses were coded on a 4-point scale. For example, students who wrote: "It shows two good-looking young Black guys wearing suits" received 4 points, while the response, "looking expensive" received only 1 point and "beer is for the working class" received no points. In this scale, students who were able to describe specific verbal or visual features of the media message to justify their assessment of the target audience demonstrated stronger analysis skills than students who used only their existing knowledge or attitudes without examining the design features of the ad. This scoring strategy reflects current scholarship in literacy education, which emphasizes the ability of students to connect their interpretive responses to textual features of a message as a key dimension of critical thinking (Scholes, 2001).

Students who participated in media literacy instruction were more likely to support their reasoning with evidence, using specific verbal or visual design features of the ad to justify their inference about the target audience. As shown in Table 7.2, there were statistically significant differences between the control group and English 11 students, with Concord students giving an average of 2.24 examples of visual or verbal evidence from the text, compared with the control group, which provided an average of only 1.63 examples to support their reasoning.

Results also showed that students in the English 11 program at Concord High School identified the target audience more narrowly as compared with the control group. Control group students were more likely to identify the ad as targeted to the broadest range of consumers. A number of statistically significant differences between the treatment and control groups reveal this pattern, as shown in Table 7.2. For example, in evaluating the age of the intended target audience, the media literacy group was less likely to identify the target audience as older. Only 24% of media literacy students identified the audience as composed of 40 to 60 year olds, compared with 33% of control group students. Similarly, 10% of media literacy students identified the target audience as over age 60, as compared with 42% of control group students. Students who received media literacy instruction were less likely to interpret the ad as targeting women consumers. There were statistically significant differences between control group students and English 11 students in assessing whether the ad targeted women, with 45% of control group students indicating this, compared with only 33% of students in the media literacy treatment.

For the largely White, middle-class high school students who participated in this study, media literacy instruction had an impact on their interpretation of how racial identity and racial identification are used by advertisers as a component of message targeting. Students in both groups recognized that African Americans were a prime target audience. But after receiving media literacy instruction, students in English 11 were much less likely to identify the ad as targeted to Whites compared with those in the control group. Students in the control group were much more likely to claim that the ad was targeted to all racial groups. Students in the media literacy treatment group were more likely to identify the target audience more narrowly. Students who received media literacy instruction were far less likely to see the message as targeted to Hispanics, Asians, or other racial groups. In analyzing students' assessments of the social class of the intended target audience, students who received media literacy instruction were also less likely to see the print beer ad as targeted to the poor. Only 24% of the media literacy students identified the beer ad as targeting poor people, compared with 43% of the control group students. It is evident that the concept of target audience was understood differently by the two groups of students.

What Techniques Were Used to Attract and Hold Attention?

Students were asked to respond in writing to this open-ended question: "List the techniques that were used to attract and hold viewers' attention." As described in the Appendix, after reading a sample of student responses, a protocol was developed to code the quality of students' open-ended response and two coders scored student work independently and blind to condition. For example, students might describe the large size of the beer can, the drops of condensation indicating its coldness, the slogan, the lettering and font choices, the facial features of the two men depicted in the ad, or the use of visual contrast and lighting. Students who recognized that an ad contains many different visual and verbal elements that are designed to attract attention and communicate meaning through symbol systems were considered to have stronger media literacy skills than those who did not identify these creative construction techniques.

Students in the media literacy treatment group identified a more construction techniques than those in the control group. As shown on Table 7.3, Concord English 11 students listed an average of 2.5 techniques compared to only 1.37 techniques listed by control group students. There were statistically significant differences in students' open-ended responses between groups, demonstrating that English 11 student could identify a greater number of verbal and visual construction techniques that were designed to attract and hold viewer attention.

What Is the Author's Purpose?

The author's purpose must always be inferred by readers—it can never be known directly. Yet strategic thinking about authorial intention is a key dimension of effective reading (Scholes, 1985). In this research, students were asked to identify the purpose of the print ad in an open-ended question. Responses were coded on a scale to reflect the different levels of understanding of how persuasion in advertising works. Three main categories

Table 7.3. Comparison of Advertising Analysis Skills.

	Control Group *n = 89*	*Treatment Group* *n = 287*
Number of techniques identified used to attract and hold viewer attention	1.37	2.50**
Identification of message purpose		
Business reason	79%	27%**
Persuasion reason	12%	49%**
Associative-Emotional reason	1%	22%**
Subtext interpretations		
Be cool	28%	51%*
Lifestyle change	22%	47%*
Drink responsibly	18%	47%*
Analysis of logo		
Don't drive drunk	61%	58%
PR strategy	26%	31%**

*p<.05
**p<.01
*** p<.001

of responses were identified after reviewing a sample of student responses. Students who wrote answers like "to sell beer" or "to make money" identified the *business* purpose of advertising. This was the "easy" answer for most students. As shown in Table 7.3, we found that 79% of control group students wrote this answer, compared to only 27% of students enrolled in English 11.

By contrast, English 11 students were much more likely to explain that advertising has *persuasive* goals. When students wrote answers like "to get people to want to drink beer," they were identifying the persuasive purpose of advertising. While 12% of the control group students gave this purpose, 49% of English 11 students wrote this as their identification of the message purpose. Only a small number of students developed a more sophisticated argument about the purpose of the ad. Some wrote statements that demonstrated that they recognized that the purpose of the ad was "to link feelings of 'coolness' with beer drinking." This is a recognition of the *associative-emotional* purpose of advertising, a phrase originally developed by Paul Messaris (1994) to describe image analysis in advertising. Students who described the ad's purpose in terms of creating a specific emotional response in viewers that could be linked to the consumption of the product were considered have more sophisticated levels of understanding of the purpose of the ad than those who merely described the ad's function to increase sales volume. As Table 7.3 shows, 1% of the control group students referred to the associative-emotional link, as compared with 22% of students enrolled in the English 11 treatment group. Clearly, the evidence shows that Concord High School students had a more sophisticated understanding of how persuasion works in advertising by creating a link between a product and a feeling.

What Is the Subtext of the Message?

Students were asked to describe the subtext of the message, defined as the unwritten meaning that the ad is trying to convey to the viewer. After reading a sample of student responses, a protocol was developed to code the three most frequently identified subtexts that students had identified: coolness, lifestyle change, and drinking responsibly. Concord English 11 students had a more sophisticated understanding of the subtext messages implied but not stated directly in the advertising message. There were statistically significant differences between the treatment group and the control group on all of the three subtext variables. As shown in Table 7.3, students in the media literacy treatment group were more likely to identify the "be cool" theme, with 51% of students identifying this subtext in the treatment group, compared with 28% in the control group. Students in the media literacy treatment group were also more likely to identify the "change your lifestyle" theme: Forty-seven percent of treatment group students identified this theme, compared to only 22% of the control group. Finally, 47% of media literacy students identified the "drink responsibly" theme compared with 18% of control group students. The experience of spending class time actively discussing persuasion, propaganda, and advertising helped students recognize and describe the unstated but implied messages in the visual imagery of contemporary advertising.

Subtext interpretation was also demanded in the question asking students to comment on the meaning of the small logo that read, "Think When You Drink." This small logo, placed on the lower right-hand corner of the ad, used the shape of a highway warning sign. Responses were coded on a 4-point scale. For example, students who wrote, "Don't drink and drive," received a lower score than students who wrote, "They want to sound responsible, plus it's good PR." The ability to recognize a legal, economic, or public relations dimension in explaining the meaning of the logo was considered a demonstration of higher levels of media literacy compared with the lower level skill of identifying the message's connection to the problem of drunk driving. This scoring strategy reflects a position common among advocates of media literacy who recognize the importance of examining the political and economic contexts in which media messages are produced (Lewis & Jhally, 1998).

There were small but statistically significant differences between control and treatment groups in the identification of this logo as part of a public relations strategy. Table 7.3 shows that 31% of students in the media literacy group identified a public relations motive, compared with 26% of control group students. Literary theorists have pointed out that subtexts can be visible through looking at patterns of "ambiguity, evasion, or overemphasis" (Eagleton, 1983, p. 155). In learning to make sense of texts that use images to communicate, subtext interpretation plays a key role. In fact, a prerequisite component of mature interpretational ability is "explicit awareness about the process by which meaning is created through the visual media" (Messaris, 1994, p. 135).

STRENGTHENING CRITICAL THINKING SKILLS BY ANALYZING ADVERTISING

This chapter has reviewed the research conducted at Concord High School designed to examine the question, How does media literacy instruction, integrated within a yearlong course in high school English language arts at Concord High School affect the development of high school students' media literacy skills as applied to advertising?

Compared to students in the control group, students who received media literacy instruction strengthened their analysis skills. First, students gained a more sophisticated understanding of the concept of *target audience*, recognizing that a single print ad is not intended to reach all possible readers or viewers, but is designed to communicate to a specific demographic group. In particular, students in the media literacy treatment appear to have gained an increased sensitivity to racial difference between minority groups. Many media literacy advocates believe that a more nuanced conceptualization of audience is a key dimension in supporting students' growth as active, socially positioned users of media texts (Buckingham, 2003b). As English teachers at Concord High School discovered, examining the relationship between authors and audiences has the potential to develop students' understandings of the cultural power of media institutions in ways that don't reduce down to simplistic conceptualizations of "brainwashing" or "ideology" (Branston, 1991).

Students in the media literacy group demonstrated the ability to support their judgments and interpretations concerning target audience using specific evidence from the advertising text. The ability to support arguments using textual evidence is one of the most central skills of literacy education at the secondary level. This study provides evidence that media literacy activities focused on analyzing advertising, when integrated into English language arts, can support the development of critical thinking skills.

Media literacy instruction leads to higher levels of awareness of the constructed nature of mass media texts. Knowledge of *media languages*—the sets of codes and conventions that are shared between producers and audiences—cannot be seen as merely neutral. The ability to recognize the constructedness of various media texts is the central concept in media literacy education, according to Tyner (1998). Such awareness is generated as students serve "cognitive apprenticeships" with teachers who emphasize the process of using active investigation to unearth meaning-making processes using the texts of everyday life, making inferences and predictions in ways that "make visible to novice learners those powerful problem-solving strategies and heuristics that more expert readers practice flexibly and strategically" (A. Lee, cited in Tyner, 1998, p. 177). Using texts (like advertisements) where students have greater social or linguistic prior knowledge may help students to master analytic skills that contribute to internalizing expert reading practices.

The findings presented in this chapter contribute to our understanding of how the use of advertising in language arts classrooms can activate adolescent critical thinking in ways that promote literacy development. As described by Robert Scholes (2005), "a proper craft of reading—including what we learn from reading poems and other literary works—can and should be used as an instrument for the serious study of *all kinds of textual objects*" (p. 215; emphasis added). In this view of literacy, the craft of reading should involve the application of critical thinking skills in relation to a wide range of print and nonprint texts, including advertising and popular culture.

By extending the concept of *cognitive defenses*, this research has defined some specific educational components of media literacy skills, which use key elements of the work of Rossiter and Robertson (1974) but are more theoretically aligned with approaches developed by British, Canadian, and Australian educators who emphasize key concepts and instructional practices designed to enhance students' critical thinking about media messages. Advertising messages are complex polysemic texts that can be used to help students recognize how authors express specific values and points of view through implied (not explicit) formulation of argument, thus strengthening inference-making skills. Through classroom instruction, English 11 teachers helped to build students' capacity as responsible readers of multimedia texts as well as twenty-first-century consumers.

Chapter 8

Media Literacy and the Development of Reading and Writing Skills

Nearly every middle school and high school English teacher knows (but doesn't like to admit) that many students in their classrooms don't comprehend what they read. They can sound out words and decode, but they can't restate the meaning of what they've read or use what they've learned to solve problems. Only 3 out of 10 eighth graders read at or above grade level, and 65% of Grade 12 students did not demonstrate reading proficiency in 2002, according to the National Assessment of Education Progress (National Center for Education Statistics, 2002). Experts note that adolescents need instruction on critical reading skills, including how to attack text in different subject areas, draw inferences, and bring background knowledge to bear in ways that make sense (Ginsberg, 2006). In 1999 the Office of Educational Research and Improvement of the U.S. Department of Education charged the Rand Reading Study Group (2004) with developing a research agenda to address the most pressing issues in literacy. Their report pointed out that all high school graduates are facing an increased need for a high degree of literacy, including the capacity to comprehend complex texts. Students in the United States are performing increasingly poorly compared to students from other countries. Most troubling of all, unacceptable gaps in reading skills persist between young people from different demographic groups despite the efforts over recent decades to close those gaps. How might media literacy contribute to the development of reading comprehension skills?

This chapter first describes the theoretical orientation of Concord's English 11 teachers in their understanding of the relationship between media literacy, critical literacy, and the practices of reading and writing. Then I reflect on teachers' approaches to integrating new literacy practices into their courses and present evidence to show how the English 11 curriculum affected the development of students' reading comprehension, critical reading, and writing skills. Evidence from teachers' descriptions of classroom practice and the results of quasi-experimental research reveals how the reading comprehension and writing skills of English 11 students fared compared to a matched control group of students who did not receive instruction in media literacy. Evidence from a teacher action research project also documents student growth in reading comprehension skills over a 5-month period. Finally, English 11 students wrote essays reflecting on the learning experience, which are examined to document students' perceptions of their own learning.

ENGLISH TEACHERS' PERSPECTIVES ON MEDIA LITERACY

Like most American teachers who begin to incorporate media analysis and media production activities in the secondary curriculum, the teachers at Concord High School did not have much of a formal understanding of the intellectual traditions of media literacy. Prior to enrolling in the summer institute I offered at Clark University, a couple of the Concord High School English teachers had been teaching film studies, but none had had any formal training in media studies. Teachers at Concord High School discovered media literacy as a result of their own reading and interests. Bob Cowan, Joanne McGlynn, and Elizabeth York remember being particularly impressed with Neil Postman's book *Amusing Ourselves to Death* (1985), which examines how television has reshaped the nature of knowledge in the twentieth century. It's important to note that media literacy was not imposed upon them by their supervisors; it bubbled up from their own perspectives, conversations, and experiences as knowledge workers. As a result, teachers at Concord High School brought an idiosyncratic mixture of perspectives about their aims and goals in integrating media analysis and media production into the secondary English curriculum.

It's not surprising that teachers stumble onto media literacy since it's unlikely that they would have encountered it in college if they were education majors. The author is aware of only a small handful of schools of education where media literacy is explored in a systematic way so that preservice teachers get more than a single class period to consider the concept. Young people with interests in education who majored in English literature, communication studies, or film studies may fare better than those who attend education schools in this regard. These individuals often have received an extensive training in the critical analysis of complex multimedia texts from various historical time periods and cultural contexts; some have had opportunities to analyze a variety of texts through a number of different theoretical perspectives. For these students, media literacy may seem a natural way to teach. Consider the case of Gregory Michie, author of *Holler if You Hear Me* (1999), a book about his first few years teaching in urban Chicago public schools. After graduating from college with an undergraduate major in communication, he spent a few years in dead-end jobs in cable television before falling into a temporary position of substitute teaching and discovering his talents as a teacher. In an effort to make a connection with his middle school students in a low-income public school who were reading far below grade level, he tried activities where students analyzed popular music and examined the bias of news reporting. As Michie describes his classroom, these activities worked to engage students with language and writing. He used his understanding of media in the lives of young people and his own critical thinking skills about the media to invent media literacy activities as a way to reach his students and pull them into a learning mode. Similarly, Concord High School's English 11 faculty made use of their own interests, experiences, and independent reading to develop an approach which integrated media literacy into the English language arts curriculum.

MULTIPLE FORMS OF LITERACY

Media literacy has such multiple roots in the communications and the education fields that there are now numerous stakeholders and interest groups, each providing a particular perspective on a complex domain. These stakeholders include parents, media professionals, teachers, librarians, technology experts, public health advocates, consumer advocates, and individuals with conservative, moderate, liberal, and radical political views. An unsuspecting teacher who Googled the phrase *media literacy* in May of 2005 would find a list of 68 million web pages. Scholars and educators have also begun to use terms such as *visual literacy, critical literacy, information literacy,* and *digital literacy* to expand the concept of literacy in order to ensure that visual, electronic, and digital forms of expression and communication are included as objects of study and analysis. With online communication and media technologies now firmly embedded at the center of the twenty-first-century cultural environment, literacy must be reconceptualized to include these new message forms and to exploit their potential to help students master the demands of reading more sophisticated texts (Kist, 2005).

Like it or not, literacy educators no longer "own" the concept of literacy. Questions about the processes of literacy are being investigated by many different scholars using a variety of theoretical and disciplinary lenses. Academic scholars in the fields of literary theory, cultural studies, history, psychology, library and information science, medicine and public health, linguistics, rhetoric, communication, and media studies have become increasingly interested in how people comprehend, interpret, critically analyze, and compose texts of various kinds (Semali, 2000).

Education practitioners (inside and outside of schools) are inventing fresh approaches for building critical thinking and communication skills in young people. Each year, a growing number of K–12 educators are using technologies to help students create their own messages—through school newspapers, online magazine articles, audio podcasts, video documentaries, and blogs (Hobbs, 2004). Business leaders, youth development specialists, federal and state education officials, community activists, and artists also have a stake in connecting media and technology to literacy education. Like the parable of the blind men and the elephant, these different groups may approach the topic from different perspectives, and as a result there are numerous, differentially nuanced visions of what these skills encompass (Hobbs, 1998; Kist, 2005; Luke, 1997; Potter, 2004; Tyner, 1998). But a review of these different perspectives shows a few common themes:

1. Visual, digital, and popular culture "texts" are just as worthy subjects for critical analysis as canonical works of classic and contemporary literature.
2. Individuals actively "read" messages of different forms, making interpretations based on their unique life experiences, cultural background, and developmental levels.
3. Instructional approaches that engage students with personally meaningful texts, authentic inquiry, and hands-on media production activities strengthen critical thinking and communication skills that directly support the development of reading, writing, speaking, and listening skills.

CRITICAL LITERACY IN ENGLISH LANGUAGE ARTS

English 11 teachers at Concord High School brought an interest in critical literacy to the design of their new course. The concept of *critical literacy* originated from scholarly traditions established by work in semiotics and cultural studies over the second half of the twentieth century. Literacy scholars have begun to define reading as not just extracting meaning from text, but the process of constructing meaning through interaction and involvement. Meaning, in this view, is understood in the context of social, historic, and power relations, not just the product of the author's intentions (Cervetti, Pardales, & Damico, 2001; Kellner, 1995). For these scholars and practitioners, texts are any form of symbolic expression used in the communication of meaning (Barthes & Keuneman, 1987). As used by critical literacy scholars, the term *critical* refers to the recognition of oppression and exploitation as embedded in texts and textual activity; critical literacy is a component of the struggle for a better society, with an explicit ideological focus on issues of inequity as related to race, gender, class, and sexual orientation (Kellner, 1995). Critical literacy education emphasizes that identity and power relations are always part of the process of composing and interpreting texts, and that these processes occur in a socioculturally and historically bound framework.

Secondary English teachers who make use of critical literacy concepts help students to examine and understand how various texts, including pictures, icons, and electronic messages (as forms of symbolic expression) are used to influence, persuade, and control people. They emphasize that reading cannot be understood as just "cracking the code" or "analyzing the author's intentions" but must be understood as an embodiment of social and political relationships. This means these teachers bring texts, topics and issues into the classroom in order to foreground sociocultural issues within a framework of power relations. English 11 teachers incorporated reading, writing, and critical viewing in ways that reflected their understanding of the identity of their students. They recognized that how an activity is defined or executed, the timing of the activity, where it occurs, and why participants are motivated to perform the activity must be considered in relation to power dynamics between teacher and student, and among learners (Rand Reading Study Group, 2004). English teachers who emphasize critical literacy see part of their mission as helping young people control their experience of the world through constructing messages to help in the transformation of society (Gee, 1996). A central component of critical literacy pedagogy is its focus on examining multiple perspectives and points of view, often through juxtaposing diverse materials, including photos, videos and other artifacts of popular culture (C. Luke, 1997; McLaughlin & DeVogel, 2004) and exploring themes related to power, identity, pleasure, and transgression (Alvermann, 2002).

Some (but not all) English 11 teachers acknowledged that they had an interest in developing critical literacy skills. For example, Mike Robb Grieco explained that he understood his job as an English teacher to be teaching students to "read the world and the word," referring to the phrase used by Freire and Macedo (1987) who described literacy's connection to issues of social justice. As the youngest teacher, Robb Grieco claims that he was brought up with an expanded conceptualization of literacy. When students were reading *Beloved* by Toni Morrison (1987), he recognized how students would wrestle with the ethical and moral questions developed through multiple points of view in this novel, and so he emphasized the question, "What's omitted from this message?" He wanted students to see that what's omitted matters—that writers design complex texts that can work on their reader on several levels. This novel features Sethe, its protagonist, who was born a slave and escaped to Ohio, but 18 years later was haunted by the memories of Sweet Home, the beautiful farm where many horrible things happened. Sethe is haunted by the ghost of her "crawling-already baby," who died nameless and whose tombstone is engraved with a single word: "Beloved."

The novel's first half has cryptic, partial, and incomplete information about Sethe's choices. When students started complaining, "This is the hardest thing I ever read," Robb Grieco responded that that was intentional—the author was inviting readers to consider just how much they know that they don't know. In responding to students' frustration, he urged them to "be cool" with the complexity and be open to tolerating ambiguity. He pointed out that, in much of ordinary life, students might not completely understand everything when they are reading media messages—it's a condition that is to be expected. Readers must use active strategies, including rereading, questioning, and predicting to build understanding. "Develop hypotheses and try to guess what's happening," he suggested. "Don't give up," he urged them. During class, Robb Grieco modeled these practices, and as students gradually began to unravel the rich symbolism of the novel, they recognized how Morrison invited her readers to enter into the consciousness of the various characters and to recognize the validity of those individuals' feelings and judgments. Robb Grieco helped students recognize the basic challenge that Morrison provided to her readers by not clearly articulating a specific moral or ethical stance toward events in the novel.

Sensitivity to this omission changes the way readers respond to the work. James Phelan (1998) explains in describing readers' response to *Beloved*, "By limiting her guidance, Morrison gives up some authorial responsibility and transfers it to the audience. By accepting that responsibility—and attending to the parameters within which Morrison asks us to exercise it—we have a more difficult and demanding but also richer reading experience. By guiding us less, Morrison gives us more. By exercising the responsibility Morrison transfers to us, we get more out of what she offers" (p. 333). Wrestling with multiple points of view and being confronted with having to position oneself in relation to ideas and respond ethically to them are dimensions of significant critical literacy.

MEASURING LITERACY OUTCOMES

As shown in previous chapters, the educators at Concord High School expanded the concept of literacy. Pragmatically, teachers were eager to discover whether their English 11 curriculum could improve reading comprehension, message analysis, and writing skills. Concord teachers knew that a few of their colleagues among the faculty were concerned that the focus on Media/ Communication was too shallow and superficial to sustain the intellectual development of some of the high-achieving students in the district. These teachers wondered how certain parents would respond, especially the ones who were concerned about their children's scores on the SAT test. How would the yearlong program of instruction affect the development of students' reading comprehension and writing skills?

To answer that question, my colleague Richard Frost and I developed a procedure to compare the reading comprehension and critical reading skills of Concord students and a control group (for research details, see Chapter 1 and Appendix; also Hobbs & Frost, 2003). To assess reading comprehension, critical reading and writing skills, students first read a newsmagazine article and then were given a series of open- and closed-ended questions about what they had read. These questions asked students to describe the main idea of the message and to identify the message's most important details, two questions which measure reading comprehension skills. To examine students' critical reading skills, they were asked to identify the purpose, target audience, construction techniques, and point of view of the newsmagazine article they had read. These questions were framed in the form that was familiar to students, the critical questions that were key ideas for the English 11 curriculum, as explained in Chapter 1 (Hobbs & Frost, 2003).

Improvement in Reading Comprehension

A one-page article entitled "Mosquitoes Get Deadly" from the September 8, 1997 issue of *Time* magazine (Kluger, 1997) was used as the stimulus for both pre- and posttests. The article concerns the spread of encephalitis among mosquitoes in Florida and the dangers of encephalitis to humans. Open-ended questions designed to measure reading comprehension asked students to identify the main ideas and supporting facts. Questions designed to measure critical reading skills asked students to identify the purpose, target audience, and point of view of the article, to describe what techniques were used to attract and hold readers' attention, and to identify at least one piece of information that was missing from the article. Figure 8.1 displays the measures.

To assess reading comprehension, students were asked to explain the main idea of the newsmagazine article. In their responses, students were to identify the "who, what, where, when, why, and how" by writing sentences to capture the main ideas of the story. For this measure of reading comprehension, scores ranged from 0 to 4. A student who wrote, "The encephalitis virus is deadly and cases have occurred in Florida and Long Island" would receive one point for identifying the location of the outbreak and another point for describing the virus as deadly, for a total of 2 points for the reading comprehension variable. A student who wrote, "States are preparing for an outbreak" or "The article was written in 1997" would receive no points. A student received 4 points for

Figure 8.1. Reading Comprehension and Analysis Activity.

Instructions: After reading the piece on mosquitoes, answer the questions below.

Put the main idea of this magazine article into a sentence or two to express the main idea. Use the WHO, WHAT, WHERE, WHEN, WHY, and HOW structure to explain the story.

What was the most memorable detail presented?

Identify three relevant questions, facts, or information that was omitted from the message.

What was the purpose of the story (check all that apply)

_____ to inform   _____ to entertain   _____ to persuade
_____ for self-expression   _____ to make money   _____ to teach

What techniques were used to attract and hold listeners' attention?

What values or points of view were represented in the message?

Who is the target audience for this message? (Place a check mark in the appropriate categories below)

_____ men   _____ Whites
_____ women   _____ African Americans
                                    _____ Asian Americans
_____ 2–11 year olds   _____ Hispanics
_____ 12–17 year olds   _____ Other
_____ 18–25 year olds
_____ 25–40 year olds   _____ poor people
_____ 40–60 year olds   _____ working-class people
_____ 60 and up   _____ middle-class people
                                    _____ upper-middle-class people
                                    _____ wealthy people

Table 8.1. Scores for Reading Comprehension, Critical Reading, and Writing Skills.

	Control Group *n = 89*	*Treatment Group* *n = 293*
Reading Comprehension		
Identification of main ideas	2.01	2.92***
Identification of supporting details	1.87	2.31**
Critical Reading		
Identification of techniques used to attract and hold reader attention	1.74	2.11***
Identification of values and point of view	1.08	1.72***
Identification of omitted information	.90	2.21***
Writing Skills		
Length of paragraph (in words)	36	72***
Holistic score of writing quality (5-point scale)	2.64	3.01

**p<.01

*** p<.001

this answer: "Scientists are worried about a possible outbreak of encefalitis [*sic*], a deadly disease carried by mosquitoes in Florida and Long Island, New York. In September 1997, scientists had located the virus in several counties and were encouraging citizens to take steps to prevent infections."

Table 8.1 shows a comparison of students in the control group to English 11 treatment group students on the skills of reading comprehension, critical reading, and writing skills. While all students showed growth from pretest to posttest, we found statistically significant differences between performance in the control group and the treatment group. Students' ability to identify main ideas improved, comparing the control group's mean of 2.01 to the treatment group's mean of 2.92. Students in English 11 were more effective in summarizing the main ideas of an informational text than those in the control group.

A second measure of reading comprehension asked students to describe the most memorable specific detail included in the article. These responses were coded to capture the level of specificity, not the specific content of students' writing. The ability to recall specific details from an informational text may be related to the interaction between readers' comprehension skills and their prior knowledge (Pressley, 1999). A student who wrote, "In 1990, eleven people died from the disease" received 3 points, the highest score. A student who wrote, "The last outbreak was in 1990" received 2 points and a student who wrote, "This happened in the United States" would receive 1 point. Incoherent or blank answers were coded as zero. By capturing the level of specificity of students' responses, this measure provided us with an indirect measure of the interaction between comprehension skills and prior knowledge. In examining the differences between the groups, we found statistically significant differences at the time of the posttest between the control group and the treatment group, with English 11 students better able to identify specific details, comparing the control group's mean of 1.87 to the treatment group's mean of 2.31. This evidence shows that English 11 students' reading comprehension skills in responding to a newsmagazine improved more substantially, compared with students in the control group.

Improvements in Critical Reading

We wanted to assess whether English 11 students demonstrated higher levels of growth in critical reading skills, including (1) recognizing creative construction techniques used in the newsmagazine article, (2) identifying the points of view depicted, and (3) generating examples of some perspectives that were omitted. As first described in Chapter 6, these concepts are central to the approach used among media literacy educators in strengthening students' ability to analyze messages.

First, students were asked to identify the creative techniques used to construct the newsmagazine article. We coded student answers on a scale from 0 to 3 points. A student received 3 points for this answer: "Using a scary headline with the word 'deadly' showing a large picture of a mosquito with a ketchy [sic] subtitle explanation." A student received 1 point for writing, "Using facts to scare you." Students also mentioned the use of statistics, the use of humor, a reference to Disney World attendees who were affected as a device to increase identification for readers, the use of the phrase "arms race" to describe the growth of infected mosquitoes, or the punchy ending that used surprising facts.

As shown in Table 8.1, Concord students were significantly better at identifying techniques used by the author to attract and hold reader attention, comparing the control group's mean of 1.74 with the treatment group's mean of 2.11. For example, Concord Grade 11 students were more likely to identify specific verbal techniques used in the newsmagazine article, especially humor, wordplay, and the use of quotations by experts. They were more likely to identify graphic design production techniques like the use of an extreme close-up of a mosquito biting a man's arm and the pull quotes to emphasize dramatic facts. For example, one student wrote, "A sense of danger is created from words like 'deadly,' 'horror' and 'mysterious.'" Another wrote: "The doctor's point of view makes mosquitoes seem important."

Secondly, students were asked to respond to the open-ended question, "What values or points of view were represented in this message?" We coded this variable on a scale from 0 to 3. For example, a student who wrote, "People must protect themselves by being more careful about spending time outdoors after dark" received 3 points. Another student wrote, "This article emphasizes the value of human life and our need to safeguard it" and also received 3 points. A student who wrote, "The doctor's point of view" received 2 points. A student who wrote, "Mosquitoes should be killed" received 1 point. English 11 students were better able to identify the points of view presented, comparing the control group's mean of 1.08 to the treatment group's mean of 1.72.

Finally, students were asked to identify ideas and information that were omitted from the newsmagazine article. This question indirectly measures a dimension of strategic, higher order comprehension because in identifying omitted information, students must be able to generate new information connected to a topic. Coders evaluated student responses on a 3-point scale, and silly, incoherent, or redundant questions, facts, or information received no points. For example, a student received 2 points for writing, "What were the ages of the two people who were killed? How to protect pets? What kind of people were most at risk?" Even though the student identified three questions, her first question was determined to have made her third question redundant, and she was not awarded an additional point. In listing omissions, students asked questions like, "Is this a problem in northern states?" and "How are Florida officials telling the public about this problem?" One student pointed out, "The perspective of parents with young children is not presented," and another wrote: "How is Disney World handling the health problem?" A student who included the question, "What do you do if symptoms appear?" would not receive a point for that question because it was specifically addressed in the newsmagazine article.

Concord students were better able to identify information that was omitted from the magazine article, which indirectly measures both students' recognition that the media message is constructed and their ability to generate ideas connected to the topic. In analyzing the omission scores, Table 8.1 shows significant differences comparing the control group's mean of .90 to the treatment group's mean of 2.21. Students in the control group were not able to generate relevant questions that were not answered in the newsmagazine article or describe specific ideas, information, and points of view that were omitted. Identifying omissions was clearly an unfamiliar task for students from the control group. By contrast, most English 11 students could list two or three ideas.

This research shows that media literacy instruction embedded within a secondary English language arts curriculum can be highly effective in meeting traditional academic goals of promoting reading comprehension and critical reading skills for nonfiction texts.

Measurable Growth in Writing Skills

We examined changes in student writing by using a single paragraph of open-ended response text generated in response to the reading comprehension questions. Writing was scored using a *holistic writing scale,* a term used for testing writing wholly through the production of writing (Cooper & Odell, 1977). Each writing sample was read by two readers who were trained in the methods of holistic evaluation. If the two readers agreed on their assessment, then the student's score was based on those two readings. If the two readers did not agree, a third reader completed the evaluation process. All writing was read "blind," which means that no names were visible to the readers during the evaluation process. No marks were placed on the writing samples during the evaluation, so that readers were not influenced by a previous reader's evaluation. The holistic writing scoring system used a 5-point scale that included evaluation of clarity, coherence, and sentence structure. Finally, we counted paragraph length in number of words, and coded the number of spelling and grammatical (not punctuation) errors.

English 11 students wrote longer paragraphs and had higher levels of overall measures of writing quality than students in the control group. English 11 students also showed substantial improvement in writing mechanics as compared with the control group. As shown in Table 8.1, they wrote longer paragraphs (mean length of 72 words as compared with 36 words). Students in the media literacy group also had higher holistic writing scores, comparing the control group mean of 2.64 to the treatment mean of 3.01, although these differences were not statistically significant because of the wide variability found among students' scores at the time of the pretest.

The treatment group's number of spelling errors declined in a statistically significant way from pretest to posttest, from 2.83 to 2.25. Students in Concord High School experienced dramatic improvements in their spelling over the course of the school year. A Pearson product moment correlation coefficient of .43 between length of paragraph and holistic quality ($p < .001$) and the coefficient of -.30 between spelling errors and holistic quality ($p < .001$) show that these data have construct validity. This evidence shows that the infusion of media literacy into the English 11 course supported students' growth as writers.

MEDIA LITERACY AND GENERAL ACADEMIC PERFORMANCE

We were concerned about whether or not students' ability to analyze media messages in print, audio, and video was a function primarily of general academic performance or a unique dimension of the learning experience. We were able to obtain grade point average (GPA) data for students at Concord High School, reflecting their academic performance at both the end of Grade 10 and Grade 11. This enabled us to examine the overall relationship between media literacy skills and overall academic performance.

A general media literacy variable was created to reflect the skills across the multimodal domains of reading, listening, and viewing. This variable consisted of a summed score based on the following eight variables: identification of creative construction techniques in reading, listening, and viewing; identification of point of view in reading, listening, and viewing; and identification of similarities and differences in television news viewing. This summary variable had a range from 17 to 0, with a mean of 8.75. A stepwise regression analysis was performed to see how much of the variance in the summed media literacy score could be simply explained by GPA. In the regression design, the criterion variable of media literacy is regressed first on GPA scores and then on pre-post treatment, this first removing the variance associated with the GPA, an indicator of academic performance, before determining if pre–post differences in media literacy are statistically significant. Regression analysis showed that after the variance due to GPA scores was removed, the pre–post treatment condition was still a statistically significant predictor of higher media literacy scores. This provides further evidence to support the validity of the media literacy variables used in this study and the robustness of students' media literacy skill development.

LEARNING THAT CONNECTS LITERACY TO LIFE

Evidence from this research demonstrates that media literacy instruction has a measurable impact on students' reading comprehension, critical reading, and writing skills. English 11 students strengthened reading comprehension and writing skills even though their exposure to print texts took a substantially different form than in a traditional literature-based class. Students in the control group used a literature-based curriculum, reading eight classic works of literature and including language arts activities including oral presentations, drama, and direct instruction in grammar and composition. English 11 students at Concord High School read classic works of literature, but they also read newspapers and magazines, analyzed scripts from documentaries, and viewed and discussed films and TV programs. We found that students' recognition of main ideas and their identification of details show that they made measurable improvements in reading comprehension. Longer paragraphs and fewer spelling errors are signs of continuing development in their writing skills.

This research also shows that students' critical thinking skills are strengthened as a result of an intensive educational intervention that explicitly uses the process of "asking critical questions about what you watch, see, and read" as an instructional framework. Students developed higher levels of ability in recognizing the complex blurring of information, entertainment, and marketing in a television news program; they identified specific construction techniques used by author and producers to get readers and viewers to pay attention to a media message; and most important, they understood how messages contain values and points of view that can be identified by examining "what's missing" from the message.

Why did English 11 with its focus on media literacy contribute to improvements in students' reading comprehension and writing skills? One obvious factor is likely to be in the area of increased motivation and interest in learning. Because students can easily see the immediate relevance of analyzing a news story about events in their own community, for example, their interest and engagement levels naturally increase. Much of the evidence from the qualitative data presented in the first part of this book demonstrate the power of student motivation, engagement, and perceived relevance to promote reading, writing, and discussion. As Elizabeth York explained, "When we reflected on our instructional program prior to implementing English 11, we realized we were pretty good at preparing students to be English majors. What we needed to do is help students to be skillful in all the messages that they are surrounded with every day of their lives." For those students who are "going through the motions" in 11th grade, a media literacy approach to language arts can awaken and inspire students, challenging them to invest the energy and commitment it takes for active development of print literacy skills to occur.

Another explanation may be a result of the curriculum's emphasis on critical thinking connected to a socially engaged learning environment. Particularly for students who are not strong readers, a sustained, yearlong focus on critical analysis that included an emphasis on seminar-style discussion with peers may have provided a scaffolding framework for students as they engaged with challenging texts that contained unfamiliar content. As we saw in Mike Robb Grieco's classroom during the teaching of the novel *Beloved*, the five critical questions served as a structural support for students' reading and inquiry as they entered into the real and imaginary worlds presented in a complex, unfamiliar text. The experience of becoming part of an active learning community may have sustained students' engaged stance in responding to complex literature and other written media.

EVIDENCE FROM TEACHER ACTION RESEARCH

English 11 teachers developed their own measures and methods for assessing whether the program was meeting its goals. For example, during the 2000–01 school year, Mike Robb Grieco and other English 11 teachers were asked by the school principal to conduct action research to discover whether the English 11 curriculum impacted reading comprehension skills. Robb Grieco used a number of strategies to support the development of students' reading comprehension skills. He involved students in close reading of key passages where students reveal and discuss how they make meaning and where and why they struggle at times. He used visual organizers for vocabulary development, which involved students in making connections between a new word and their own prior knowledge, beyond the standard dictionary definition of a word. He used reading quizzes and tests, analytical essay writing on readings, and creative writing and projects. These activities inspired students to construct original works using specific techniques and voices that required depth in audience response.

With a background in teaching English to second-language learners, Robb Grieco approached the task of designing an action research project using concepts from linguistics. In exploring how students learn a new language, researchers examine surface-level comprehension and deep structures. At the surface level, meaning can be classified into two broad categories: understanding the denotative meaning of words and understanding the connotative meanings of words. *Denotative meaning* is the meaning of words given in the dictionary, while *connotative meaning* is the communicative value of an expression, over and above its purely denotative meaning. Connotative meanings reflect the real-world experiences that people associate with an idea. At the deep structure level, meaning can also be divided into two categories: contextual meaning and pragmatic meaning. Unlike the surface meaning of a single word, *contextual meaning* is realized at the sentence level and is the meaning expressed by a sentence associated with its context. Contextual meaning (often called *literal meaning*) is not decided by the word itself but by the context in which the whole sentence functions. *Pragmatic meaning* (often called *inferential meaning*) is communicated in the feelings and attitudes of the writer. It is the writer's intended unspoken or unwritten meaning (Sheng, 2000).

Using these concepts to guide his action research, Robb Grieco selected two articles from *Brill's Content* magazine written by Mike Pride, the editor of the Concord *Monitor*. Students read one at pretest and another at posttest. Each article shared a common format and focus: a two-page spread, two visuals, standard font with decontextualized quotations, and the content focused on the responsibility of local newspapers to generate discussion of community issues and an exploration of how those issues should be framed. Robb Grieco composed five questions to assess students' vocabulary comprehension, literal understanding, inference-making, application outside the immediate context, and an open-ended opinion question evaluating students' ability to support opinions with evidence from the text and prior knowledge. An example of a vocabulary question was: "In the passage, 'When I cooled off, I realized that persuasion is always preferable to coercion,' what does *coercion* mean?" An example of an inferential question was: "Mike Pride states his belief that a 'code of silence' is a problem at Concord. Define the 'code of silence' to which he refers." Students were allowed 60 minutes to read the article, then read and answer questions. Students were able to refer to the text in answering questions. Each question was assessed on a scale of 1 to 5 points. The teacher summed students' responses by category and compared the averages in each area of comprehension.

Students showed dramatic evidence of substantial growth in reading skills over a 5-month period. As shown in Table 8.2, students' vocabulary development improved from 60% to 73%. Their ability to make inferences jumped from 38% to 68%. Students' responses on open-ended questions improved from 50% to 72%. In reflecting on the results he found, the teacher explained that improvement was most likely a result of writing instruction where students "were constantly asked to illustrate their thinking with specific examples to reveal their analytical processes to their readers."

STUDENTS' REFLECTIONS ON THEIR LITERACY LEARNING

Students had their own ideas about the English 11 course, and some teachers invited students to share their perceptions of the learning experience. In one class, students wrote essays describing their experience in English 11. Most students acknowledged that the course had increased their skepticism about many aspects of contemporary social life. One student wrote, "I find myself wondering about the intentions of things that in the past I would have ignored or absorbed for face value. Skepticism forces me to engage intellectually with all media I encounter every day." This skepticism seemed related to having learned that all media texts are constructed. According to another student, "We've also learned that people who report information to us often construct their own personal view while reporting to viewers, which complicates your ability to form your own opinion on issues, due to the media distorting facts as they report them."

The experience of reading challenging literature that presented a multitude of distinct voices and perspectives helped students develop some reflective appreciation for the critical thinking skills they were developing as readers.

Table 8.2. Teacher Action Research on Reading Comprehension Skills.

Reading Skill	Pretest n = 12	Posttest n = 12
Vocabulary in context	60%	73%
Literal understanding	91%	91%
Inferences	38%	68%
Application (beyond context)	10%	72%
Open-ended informed opinions	50%	72%

Note. Data collected by Michael Robb Grieco.

One student explained that *As I Lay Dying* "forced me to acknowledge a simple but crucial fact: Novels are deliberate constructions." This idea expanded as the year progressed to include broadcast journalism, advertising, newspapers, and films. This student continued to explain that she found that she had to initially doubt the statements of Faulkner's narrators until she could establish some sort of proof that they were real. She had to be persistent in deciphering truths from elaborations, actual events from imagined ones, and the characters' lived experiences from her own perceptions of life. This stance of reading with an engaged, critical eye carried over into her reading of Toni Morrison's *Beloved,* and Ken Kesey's *One Flew Over the Cuckoo's Nest.* In reading *Cuckoo's Nest,* she confronted her own discomfort reading from the point of view of the narrator who is likely insane. She explained, "Though I considered myself a critical thinker prior to the course, I don't think this label fit my reading style at the time. Due to the monotony of prior English classes, I had been trained to passively read a book with a ridiculously obvious theme or message, come up with a thesis statement, and crank out a paper. These books made that impossible."

Students recognized that authors compose media messages using creative rhetorical and construction techniques to accomplish their purposes. In writing about a lesson on *The Perfect Storm,* one student wrote, "Creators of books and movies have to make critical decisions about how to construct a story just like newspaper editors and TV news directors." Other students articulated the recognition that discovering that media messages are constructions changed their position as readers. One student wrote, "The truth is at the beginning of the year I knew very little about the mechanics of media; I had no idea about how it was constructed. We spent time examining all kinds of media: books, magazines, television, and movies. The one thing they all had in common was they were constructions. Everything around us is trying to sell something, be it an idea, a product, or a philosophy."

It's clear that, like their teachers, the teens in English 11 wrestled with doubt—when that which is taken-for-granted as trustworthy is shaken by new understandings. One student asked, "How do you know when you can trust the media, the government, your best friend?" Another wondered, "If all media was [*sic*] carefully assembled to make me think a certain way, could I trust it [*sic*]? It is much better to tend to disbelieve than trust wholeheartedly. In America today, those who trust are manipulated, while those who doubt obtain answers." Another commented that he often finds himself doubting what he reads in the paper or sees on television, because he recognizes that the media use gossip and intrusion to spark the interest of readers and viewers as part of a business strategy. Because life requires people to make decisions based on the quality of information they receive, it's a healthy and necessary position for young people to be able to recognize that messages are socially constructed products, not mirror images of reality. It's a life skill that can be learned with guidance from English language arts teachers, whose central focus is not only to pass on a literary heritage to the next generation, but who can engage students in dynamic learning experiences that deeply examine how meaning is constructed through symbolic forms of expression and communication.

Conclusion

The Future of Media Literacy in Schools

When 21-year-old Alyssa Spellman amazed the New Hampshire judges with her poise, attractiveness, and vocal talent, she won the prestigious title of Miss New Hampshire 2004. As the tiara-crowned winner of the 58th annual Miss New Hampshire Scholarship Program, she received a $20,000 scholarship award. Alyssa, then a junior at Emerson College in Boston, had wowed the audience with her vocal talents displayed in her performance of "The Laughing Song" from *Die Fledermaus*. Like the other Miss America candidates, she was required to have a particular platform issue about which to raise public awareness when touring across the nation. As she went on to compete for the title of Miss America, Alyssa Spellman became the first Miss America contestant in the history of the pageant to take media literacy as her platform issue. Alyssa, who graduated with honors from Concord High School in 2001, was a member of the Alliance for a Media Literate America (AMLA), a national organization for media literacy. Clearly, her experience as a student in English 11 had an impact on her. Recognizing that media texts, tools, and technologies play a central role in the lives of children and young people, she wanted to increase public awareness about the value of media literacy as an essential life skill.

This chapter reviews and summarizes what I have learned about media literacy education as it was implemented at Concord High School. Alyssa Spellman is but one of the more than 3,000 students who experienced English 11 at Concord High School over the past 9 years. With 18 different teachers teaching the course over that time period, it is unlikely that any two students had exactly the same learning experience. But in considering the impact of the program on students, it is important to recognize the contributions made by students, texts, instructional practices, teachers, school structure and leadership, and the community. It is also important to reflect upon issues that arose in the research process, examining the challenges and opportunities for developing an expanded conceptualization of literacy among English language arts educators in the twenty-first century.

LEARNING OUTCOMES

As I have shown in this book through both quantitative and qualitative evidence, students measurably strengthened their comprehension skills as readers, listeners, and viewers in responding to print, audio, visual, and video texts. They increased the ability to restate the main ideas they encountered in informational texts. In analyzing messages, students demonstrated the ability to recognize the complex blurring of authorial intention and purpose as texts may simultaneously strive to inform, to persuade, to entertain, and to make money for their authors. They acquired a more focused appreciation of the concept of audience, appreciating that media messages (while they may be read or viewed by anyone) are designed to appeal to particular audiences. They learned that authors hold an imaginary reader in their minds as they compose, considering how to connect their goals to the reader's own agenda. In learning about advertising, students gained a deeper understanding of how messages use ambiguity and identification to create emotionally resonant symbolic links between products, needs, and feelings. The research reported in this book has demonstrated that, overall, students developed a more sophisticated understanding of how authors compose messages to convey meaning through the use of language, image, and sound and how readers respond with their own meaning-making process as they interpret messages.

Because they developed skills of analyzing messages using both texts that were highly familiar (like TV shows, movies, popular music, and advertising) as well as with unfamiliar materials (like literature and informational texts), they gained the ability to understand and use structural knowledge about a wide range of genres, forms, and message types. Students' critical thinking skills were enhanced because they were able to employ a simple and clear set of concepts, the key concepts of media literacy, which provided a heuristic framework.

As English 11 students explored the news media, they discovered the power of communication to shape the public's understanding of social reality. They recognized how the news media shapes messages through a variety of different techniques and that these techniques mean that news media messages are never objective, but always partial, selective, and incomplete. But they also learned how to take action in responding to press coverage of a news event, discovering the power of "talking back" to the news media and learning, in the process, about some of the responsibilities and obligations of citizenship.

Rather than see "the media" as a monolithic entity, students in English 11 discovered that, as Toto revealed to Dorothy in *The Wizard of Oz*, media messages are not the work of an all-powerful wizard, but created by teams of rather ordinary people who are doing a demanding job, making both good judgments and mistakes often under challenging day-to-day circumstances.

Students gained power as communicators, developing their skills of speaking, writing, and media production. Students had many opportunities to use language, images, and sounds in expressing a message. The evidence presented in this book shows that students' writing improved because they had repeated opportunities to write about subjects that they cared about, where they could bring their confidence, knowledge, and personal interests to the writing process. The pleasures they took in popular culture were respected by peers and teachers, so they gained confidence in reflecting upon their behaviors as media consumers. Through regular and sustained opportunities for dialogue, students realized that they were shaping their own learning experience through what they, their peers, and their teacher each contributed to the quality of conversation. When writing and speaking, students got opportunities to share their opinions or present their point of view, but they were continually challenged to use evidence and reasoning to support their ideas. In the absence of school access to video production equipment, many English 11 students were able to use their own home equipment to compose a message using a combination of language, images, sound, and special effects.

Students gained a deeper appreciation for the value of teamwork and collaboration by participating in activities that involved small-group problem solving and the exercise of imagination. They developed respect for the contributions of others, coming to see learning not as a competitive game but as an intensely social and interactive process. Through the process of asking critical questions, their curiosity was stimulated, and they grew as independent learners. Many students experienced the genuine thrill of research and discovery that comes from seeking knowledge. These learning outcomes are consistent with what many school reform advocates describe as the key elements of active, engaged learning (Sizer, 1996).

THE COMMUNITY AS LEARNING ENVIRONMENT

The outcomes just described were made possible because of the learning environment at Concord High School. Community values, local news media, school leadership, and the structural dimensions of the high school all had an influence on the implementation of the new curriculum. The community's support of the new initiative reflected some fundamental values, including the overall conceptualization of curricular change. Curriculum reform was understood to be the responsibility of the faculty, not something to be imposed upon them from above. In some communities, curriculum reform is viewed as a signal that there is a "problem" in the schools that needs to be "solved." In Concord, New Hampshire, parents and school leaders viewed curriculum reform as a necessary, healthy, and vital process. There was little of the tension that exists in some schools when curricular reform efforts make teachers feel that their teaching practices are being criticized (Muncey & McQuillan, 1996; Sizer, 1984). Among Concord school leaders, there was a shared expectation that the faculty could be trusted to design a new course and implement it effectively. The community believed that the goals of both relevance and rigor could be partnered in the new English 11 course in media/communication.

Having a high-quality local newspaper in the community provided students and teachers with an important textual resource, but more important, the newspaper's values reflected the community's values to reveal key dimensions of why media literacy is so well supported in the community. The newspaper regularly takes on sensitive and controversial issues that are relevant to young people, like the debate at Concord High School over the school policy prohibiting the use of alcohol, tobacco, or drugs by school athletes. The newspaper brought to public attention the code of silence among parents who were aware that their children were violating the policy, and through a series of meetings coordinated by the parent–teacher organization, it was possible for the community to discuss this formerly taboo topic and initiate possibilities for making changes (Pride, 2000). And in Concord, newspaper readers are not just clipping supermarket coupons. The *Monitor* publishes a much larger proportion of letters to the editor than most newspapers its size. According to editor Mike Pride (2006), "Readers are so outspoken, well-spoken, sharp, cranky, warm, funny and thoughtful that their letters get high readership. Every survey we have ever done confirms the popularity of the letters columns" (p. 1). He receives more than a dozen letters each day, an indication of how many citizens in the community have adopted the stance of the "active reader" that teachers in English 11 tried to promote.

Over the 9 years in which I conducted my research, I never encountered the kind of mean-spirited muttering about school leadership or tempestuous internal politics that are commonplace in many schools. While I'm certain there must have been some of that, English 11 teachers generally described school leaders as supportive and helpful. For example, I was informed about how assistant principals helped teachers handle students who were disruptive, emotionally or behaviorally troubled, and even those who came to class late. When students did not complete work, there was a system in place for communicating with parents. Teachers did not have to lower their expectations for students or accommodate the level of work completed by those students who clearly would not pass the course. And interviews with the school principal revealed deep respect for the professionalism of the English faculty and no sense of wanting to control or orchestrate the curricular reform process. School leaders were attentive to the English 11 course. I remember that the school principal once visited a class that I was also visiting, giving us all the sense that he valued the work. School leaders also set high expectations for teachers, encouraging them to document student learning through teacher action research.

Block scheduling, heterogeneous grouping, and common planning time were three key structural elements that made it possible for English 11 to be a success at Concord High School. Researchers have found that, in many schools, it is hard to effect curricular reform because of the requirements for changing both the structure of the school day and the roles and responsibilities of teachers and students within that structure, creating a situation with too many different kinds of change occurring too fast (Muncey & McQuillan, 1996). At Concord High School, the school had already embraced heterogeneous grouping and block scheduling, two structural changes that affected teachers' roles in the classroom. English 11 teachers had already accommodated to the new demands placed on them resulting from these reforms, particularly in the areas of designing lessons and activities to meet the needs of diverse individual learners and using a variety of instructional methods within a longer block of time. As a result, when challenged to incorporate visual, media, and popular culture texts, tools, and technologies alongside literature in the English 11 Media/Communication course, they could focus on and develop the course content and ideas. And while most English 11 teachers noted that the common planning time of one class period per week was not enough time for meaningful discussion to occur, it did enable teachers to share experiences and resources.

THE CLASSROOM LEARNING ENVIRONMENT

English 11 teachers used a wide variety of texts, themes, and instructional practices in the classroom. They selected diverse print material, including classic works of literature, contemporary fiction, young-adult literature, essays, nonfiction books, magazine articles, news stories, opinions, and works of criticism. They selected videos including documentaries, fiction films, TV news and informational programs, entertainment shows, and advertising. They made active use of the Internet both for finding resource materials for their students and as a tool for independent student research.

The course content and ideas centered on some key themes:

1. The social role of the storyteller and the dimensions and devices of storytelling
2. The use of language and images as tools for social control and the exercise of power
3. The complex relationship of media messages in respect to truth, memory, and history and the nature of media representations as inevitably partial, selective, and incomplete
4. The social contexts of communication and the responsibilities of individuals as participants in community life

Because these themes are so broad, teachers sometimes felt that the English 11 course encompassed too much terrain for them to navigate effectively with their students. But because teachers used a simple structural heuristic (the key concepts of media literacy and the five critical questions described in Chapter 1), they could approach these themes in ways that made it easy for students to engage with the ideas. Even the least academically talented teen can attempt to answer the question, "What creative production techniques are used to attract and hold attention?" The practice of close reading of a text—looking at key passages and examining images, language, and ideas carefully—strengthened students' literacy development.

Through an interrelated sequence of writing, talking, reading, viewing, and research experiences, English 11 students discovered how ideas build upon ideas. As one scholar has put it, "Successful class discussion . . . builds a network of understandings as each piece of new information sequentially transforms and expands given information into new understandings" (Nystrand, 1997, p. 90). English 11 teachers were effective in promoting meaningful dialogue in the classroom because they started on familiar ground with media texts, tools, and technologies where students could actively share their expertise and opinions with confidence. As they introduced new and challenging materials and activities, teachers used the key concepts and critical questions to help students negotiate the meaning-making process. Through the use of texts from both high culture and popular culture, students wrestled with ideas and experienced the struggle of contrasting perspectives. Were politicians as manipulative and shallow as the ones depicted in the film *Wag the Dog*? Or were they more like the socially committed people depicted on the pages of the Concord *Monitor* and the *New York Times*? These were not questions that could be answered by their teachers—students had to work out their own interpretations through active discussion and reflection with teachers, family, and peers.

POLITICAL IDEOLOGY IN THE CLASSROOM

Contemporary scholarship in media education has long questioned the value of an approach that positions students as victimized by mass media culture and ignores or trivializes the genuine pleasures and polysemous meanings of media in everyday life (Alvarado & Boyd Barrett, 1992; Buckingham & Sefton-Green, 1994). English teachers who explore the topics of advertising, propaganda, and persuasion in a sociopolitical context usually do this without formal training, and there is often a lack of consensus among colleagues about what to emphasize. Pointing out the implicit ideological formulation of the propaganda model as taught by some teachers, Canadian scholar Robert Morgan (2003) writes: "Media are the active force in the relationship: the media do—they construct, act upon, manipulate, seduce, influence identity, shape culture; students, on the other hand, are done to—acted upon, manipulated, exposed or vulnerable to—are victims in essence" (p. 118).

For some who claim to be teaching media literacy, *deconstruction* or close reading of texts is positioned as simply the process of exposing strategies of media manipulation. In this drastically simplified conceptualization, learning about media propaganda automatically transforms a person from passive to active and from emotional to rational. For these educators, media literacy is sometimes positioned as an antidote to the evils of consumer capitalism. But according to Buckingham (2003c), "To imply that 'ideology' will be overcome simply through the application of conscious rationality is little more than wishful thinking" (p. 66).

As shown in Chapter 3, some English 11 teachers valued the opportunity to emphasize the processes of critical analysis as a means to counter the negative influence of the media in the lives of adolescents. Although they did not explicitly describe their work as protecting students from media influence or position themselves oppositionally to "Big Media," English 11 teachers had genuine concerns about the impact of media on young people. For example, Bob Cowan believed that the media did damage to his students and that the course's value was in exploring "how media texts connect to issues of tolerance, respect, issues of community, and living a healthy life." In describing her goals, Joanne McGlynn talked about her concerns about students' apathy, which she believed had been cultivated by positioning students as consumers and not citizens. She said, "The best thing that would happen would be that all the kids in the class would feel challenged. And at the end of the year, they would all be confident in their critical analysis skills. And not only would they be confident, but they would be less numb. That lack of awareness would be broken through." McGlynn also wrestled with these questions about numbness and awareness herself—in her own political beliefs—at the same time she was exploring them with her students. As the most politically active of the English 11 teachers, she had been instrumental in bringing Bill Clinton to Concord High School, twice, when he ran for president in 1992 and 1996. Watching the media spectacle unfold around the Monica Lewinsky scandal, she said, "It's really complicated. But what we want is engagement. And yet, when you look at the world around you, you wonder, how is it possible to be engaged when what this looks like is a circus. And the only role that makes sense is a spectator—then disengagement actually seems quite functional, in a manner of speaking. But I don't want them to become cynics."

A number of English 11 teachers were challenged by the many ways in which ideological issues regularly entered into classroom discussions. Some delighted in the opportunity to explore issues of power, social justice and inequity, while others had real reservations. For example, Tim Doughtery taught English 11 for only one year—he did not enjoy teaching the course. In reflecting on his experiences, he wondered about whether the course really was an "English" course because the emphasis on critical and cultural analysis made him uneasy. He said, "I felt like I was giving short shrift to the author's message." In deciding not to continue teaching the course, he concluded that the issues of power and politics, while important, were not appropriate topics to include in an English course, which he viewed as needing to center on the power of literature and language, not the sociopolitical context or cultural dimensions of messages. When media texts and literary texts are examined within a single course, there was a loss of disciplinarity that was troubling to Doughtery, who said, "We diminish both fields to assume that they belong in the same space." James Doneski also voiced concerns about the course taking on a more "civics class flavor" and sometimes found the partisan politics in the news to be tiresome.

At Concord High School, teachers' own complex political beliefs and ideologies inevitably entered into their teaching—in the selection of texts, in the topics and issues they emphasized, and in the instructional methodologies they employed. It is a deeply held belief among many English teachers that literature has a broadly humanizing effect on readers, while media texts are presumed to have negative effects. "If literature teaching is primarily about developing students' receptiveness to something which is seen as fundamentally good, a great deal of media teaching is encouraging students to resist or 'see through' something which is seen as fundamentally bad" (Buckingham, 1992, p. 127).

Power and ideology have always been intertwined with literature. As one literary scholar put it, "From Percy Bysshe Shelley to Norman N. Holland, literary theory has been indissociably bound up with political beliefs and ideological values" (Eagleton, 1983, pp. 169–170). But most approaches to teaching reading and writing in secondary schools stay far away from an examination of how texts work in maintaining or challenging the social status quo. American teachers are not especially unique in this regard. Internationally, Andrew Hart and his colleagues have explored the lack of comfort that secondary-level English teachers have when exploring social, economic, and political issues. In a book which presents case studies of the implementation of media literacy among secondary teachers in six countries, many examples showed that English teachers avoided explorations of the political or economic dimensions of media texts. In Northern Ireland, for example, high school English teachers were uncomfortable exploring the political/religious ideologies represented in their mass media and deliberately did not use local newspapers as study objects (Collins, 1998). In Western Australia, a high school English teacher used *Gallipoli* (1981) to explore changes in the representation of Australian identity, without examining the political or economic contexts in which the film was produced, particularly the role of Rupert Murdoch in producing the film and orchestrating the expensive media campaign that accompanied it (Quin, 1998). It may be that English teachers focus on textual analysis and only rarely explore the institutional contexts of media production in part because of their own lack of knowledge, training, and experience in this area (Hart, 1998).

At Concord High School, English teachers had different levels of familiarity with sociopolitical approaches to examining texts in context, and as a result they brought a wide range of sometimes divergent perspectives into their work. But there was no sense of a moral, political, or ideological litmus test operating among the English 11 faculty. Teachers who didn't care to explore the topic of media ownership were free not to do so, and there was no "party line" about what to teach about media texts, media economics, or media industries. Teachers were free to tackle the complex themes of the course in the ways that best suited their interests and talents. There was a high level of respect and autonomy among faculty colleagues, even though there were divergent perspectives among them on the ideological issues explored in the course. This may have been one of the elements that contributed to the long-running success of the course.

MEDIA LITERACY AND THE INTERNET

In examining how the concept of media literacy relates to the Internet, Sonia Livingstone (2003) has pointed out that it may still be too soon for the connection to be fully understandable. There are still huge socioeconomic disparities in the conditions under which the Internet can be accessed by children and young people in the United States and around the world. And while competencies have been clearly articulated for analyzing print, visual, and electronic media, no parallel conceptualization of Internet-related analytical skills have fully emerged. The new kinds of texts and social interactivity that are emerging on the Internet (i.e., blogging, podcasting, webcomics, IM/chat, and games of all sorts) are still not established enough to have acquired a clear sense of genre; norms and expectations for these different message forms are fluid. There is also the simultaneous development of the rapidly expanding use of cell phones and handheld devices among adolescents for purposes of expression and communication. Not surprisingly, it was not yet clear to English 11 teachers how media literacy might be applied to these new media texts, tools, and technologies.

As we learned in previous chapters, when educators at Concord High School did approach the challenge of incorporating web content into English 11, they focused on the ability to evaluate the authority, credibility, and quality of informational texts available online. Because the Internet removes the filters between authors and audiences, teaching users to question the messages they receive online is crucial. Teachers at Concord High School focused on the challenges of *source evaluation*, looking at authorship, purpose, and point of view. Specific techniques they used included studying the URL, looking at where hyperlinks lead, and seeing what other sources say about the author (Barker, 2005). In reading texts online, a skillful reader asks, for example, why links are made from certain points and not others, where those links lead, and what values are entailed in such decisions (Burbules, 1998). Information and communication technologies can't be treated simply just as a digital text, to be analyzed the same way that print and visual media texts are read.

There are unique qualities of the Internet that need investigation: for example, the nature of interactivity, the ability to have both synchronous and asynchronous communication, and the rise of communally constructed texts that are built on the principle of distributed intelligence. The participatory culture that is embedded in the current media landscape is global, multimodal, mobile, and collaborative, with sharp differences between generations in terms of access to knowledge, cultural tastes and interests, and forms of participation and learning. As a result, students need a range of new knowledge, competencies, and skills including playfulness, navigation, negotiation, teamwork, and judgment (Jenkins, 2006). But like many American teachers, Concord High School teachers still lack basic tools (including the ability to access the Internet in their classrooms and project the screen so all students can see it). They can take students to the school's computer lab for a special activity, of course, but without the technological infrastructure available in the classroom, it will take time to incorporate "new media literacy" into their English 11 course.

MEDIA LITERACY AND EDUCATION POLICY

This book has aimed to paint a picture of what media literacy education looks like when integrated into the context of one high school English language arts program. While many educators and scholars have urged that media literacy be integrated within the K–12 curriculum, it has been difficult to capture exactly what the concept of *integration* entails. This book has shown how media literacy enables educators to be more responsive to the social contexts in which learning occurs and emphasize the development of critical thinking skills that help students think more deeply about subject matter.

At the beginning of the twenty-first century, English language arts educators now confront deep divisions between those who emphasize mastery in skills development, those who emphasize the cultural heritage model based on the "great books," and those who emphasize a process-oriented approach that draws from research on the writing process, reader response theories, and social theories of reading comprehension (Peters & Wixson, 2003). In many schools, the schisms that exist between these different perspectives have led to ill-defined curricula that contribute to poor student performance. When media literacy has been put forward as yet one more approach to English language arts, it is not surprising that school leaders and classroom practitioners just shrug their heads and mutter, "Don't give me another thing to have to cover, there's already too much to do." But the evidence presented in this book has shown that the inclusion of media literacy is highly consistent with efforts to streamline and focus English language arts curriculum along the following themes:

1. Genre, craft and the conventions of symbolic expression
2. The value of literature for its ability to bring "great ideas" into the classroom
3. Elements of effective communication
4. Skills, strategies, and processes of meaning making

Policy makers, educators, and researchers operate in very different worlds. Each group has only a partial and incomplete understanding of the others' incentives, constraints, and day-to-day work (McDonnell, 2005). At present, educational policy makers want to be able to use educational testing to provide unbiased and comprehensive data about student achievement. The value of educational testing and accountability is a deeply held cultural belief in the United States, but "history shows that testing alone, in itself, is unlikely to bring about major education improvement" (Haertel & Herman, 2004, p. 29). Regardless, some educators in the United States have felt increasingly controlled by standardized instructional planning, supervision, and evaluation; these teachers feel they "can't afford the time" to include media literacy because of the pressure to prepare students for achievement tests. This has led to an erosion of teacher professionalism and autonomy, leading to a decline in the quality of education for all students (Ruth, 2003).

Another deeply held cultural belief may hold some promise to promote educational policy that will increase the integration of media literacy into the English language arts curriculum—the belief that technology is beneficial to support student learning. Dialogue and debate are building national and international consensus among policy makers, educators, and scholars concerning the relationship between literacy, technology, and education. For example, in the spring of 2003, the Partnership for 21st Century Skills, a public-private organization formed with support from the U.S. Department of Education and the business community, held a forum in Tucson, Arizona, with leaders in education, universities, nonprofit organizations, and business. The focus of the meeting was to create a consensus concerning the definition of "21st-century learning skills" and to map out some effective strategies that could help educational leaders implement these skills with children and young people in American public schools. One of the most noticeable elements of this meeting was the wide range of terminology used to capture the array of competencies required for effective communication in a technologically mediated cultural environment. *Higher order thinking skills, media literacy, ICT literacy, communication skills* and *digital literacy* were only a few of the many terms used to describe those competencies required for life in an information- and media-saturated society. Participants also identified the need to link core subjects and basic skills to a "21st-century context" to help students discover the relevance and value of new skills and knowledge to the world outside the classroom. As demonstrated in this book, when educators help students to recognize the connections between their schoolwork and their lives outside the classroom, they build student engagement, motivation, and attitudes in ways that ultimately strengthen academic performance.

WHY MEDIA LITERACY MATTERS

As Livingstone (2003) has put it, "A literate society is surely a society of knowledgeable, critical, engaged people who will demand channels for participating in and influencing cultural, political, and social institutions" (p. 25). Literacy has personal, social, and institutional functions in contemporary society. Literacy can no longer be conceptualized as an isolated set of practices involving decoding, phonemic awareness, five-paragraph essays, and reading quizzes. Media literacy can no longer be conceptualized as protecting youth from television's "background radiation of the social and intellectual universe" (Postman, 1985, p. 79). There is a need for people to take greater responsibility for their use of all texts—print, visual, electronic, and digital media. Making informed choices, questioning texts, composing and sharing ideas using various symbol systems, tools, and technologies, and fully engaging in the practices of citizenship—these are key dimensions of literacy in an information age. This book has used compelling quantitative and qualitative evidence to show that there are specific ways in which young people can be prepared for the demands of life in a technologically sophisticated and communication-rich cultural environment. There are institutional structures within schools and community values that can support the work of educators who want students to be media literate. Educators interested in bringing this new vision of literacy to future generations should study closely and learn from the experiences of teachers who have been on the front lines. As they continue to wrestle to discover new ways to engage and challenge students, educators will meet the challenge with imagination, dedication, and hard work.

Research Design and Methodology

This research used a mixed-methods research design, combining qualitative and quantitative research methods. Each research method provided insights on the complex learning environment at Concord High School.

QUALITATIVE INQUIRY

Qualitative research was used primarily to gather information to document the nature of the instruction used in English 11 and to learn more about how teachers and students perceived the learning experience as they implemented media literacy into a high school English language arts curriculum. This book strives to capture the lived experiences of Concord High School teachers in order to help both practitioners and scholars understand the opportunities and challenges of this work.

I made many visits to Concord High School between 1998 and 2005, conducting interviews with teachers and students and observing classroo During the first three years of this study, I made three daylong visits during a school year; in later years, I would visit only once or twice a year, with occasional email and phone conversations with teachers. During my visits, I spent the bulk of my time interviewing teachers. Teachers were asked to describe the lessons and activities that they had just completed or were currently working on with their English 11 students. This approach provided indirect evidence about classroom practice and curriculum content. I used the questions shown in Figure 1.3 to guide my inquiry, as these questions invited teachers to reflect on broader issues related to student learning and community impact.

Throughout the data collection process, it was important for me to clarify my role in relation to teachers at Concord High School, both for my own work as a teacher-researcher and for teachers who occasionally sought guidance about their work. I had first met three Concord teachers through a staff development experience I offered at Clark University, entitled "Teaching the Humanities in a Media Age." The design of their curriculum was undoubtedly influenced by some of the ideas encountered there. Three of the lesson plans described in this book bear a deep imprint of my own ideas: five critical questions, the realism continuum, and the Frankenstein activities were lessons I had demonstrated. In my ongoing discussions with the staff, I identified some tensions between my role as researcher and as teacher educator. Throughout the process, it was challenging to resist the temptation to coach or mentor teachers. On a couple of occasions I found myself inadvertently suggesting a lesson plan, activity, or book in response to some part of an interview with a teacher. When one teacher thanked me for an idea I had mentioned in a previous interview and told me how it had worked in the classroom, it heightened my awareness of the complexity of my own dual identity as teacher-researcher.

Whenever I went to Concord, I tried to visit at least two English 11 classrooms, observing a classroom activity or interviewing students. This resulted in a data set that included 21 hours of interviews, which were professionally transcribed. I maintained a notebook when interviewing teachers without an audiotape or in situations where excessive noise limited my ability to audiotape. In these notebooks, I included my observations of classroom activity and student behavior, and made other observations related to the overall climate of the school. In using the qualitative data in this book, I make extensive use of teachers' and students' ideas, indicating this by the use of direct quotation. In a few cases, in order to improve readability, when teachers described the comments, ideas, or behavior of their students, I use direct quotation even though some of these comments represent a teacher's description of a student's idea and not one that I myself directly observed.

QUANTITATIVE INQUIRY

In this book I also present the results of quantitative inquiry, which was used in order to better understand changes in student performance over time and to support the development of theory building. For social science research in both media studies and education, the guiding principles include the requirements to pose significant questions that can be investigated empirically, link research to theory, use methods that permit direct investigation of the question, provide a coherent chain of rigorous reasoning, and replicate and generalize (Feuer & Towne, 2006). In designing an approach to measure changes in student performance over time, I relied on a theoretical model of media literacy based on concepts from media studies and education. That included an emphasis on examining students' reception of media texts, looking at reception from a multimodal perspective, including print, audio, visual, and electronic materials, and conceptualizing students as active readers who use their prior knowledge, attitudes, and life experiences in the message interpretation process (Bazalgette, 1991; Buckingham, 2003b).

The research design used a quasi-experimental nonequivalent-groups design, structured like a pretest–posttest experiment, but without random assignment to groups. Because all students in the school district participated in the English 11 course at Concord High School, it was impossible to use random assignment to measure the impact of this instructional treatment on student learning. Quasi-experimental designs are common in education research (Babbie, 2004), but they have been critiqued by both advocates of single-subject research and advocates of qualitative research, who point out methodological limitations (Kennedy, 1997; Richardson, 1994). However, nonequivalent research designs are still a powerful tool for understanding the effectiveness and impact of new instructional interventions. In true experiments, participants are randomly assigned to treatment conditions. In quasi experiments, researchers often use students from intact classes or schools as the treatment sample and try to find a relatively comparable group of students from other classes or schools to serve as the comparison sample (Cook & Campbell, 1979). In the most frequently used type of quasi-experiment, researchers typically assess students on a battery of pretest measures to ensure equivalence between the experimental group and the control group; quasi-experimental designs are strengthened when researchers can prove that the groups were highly similar at pretest time. However, even when control and experimental groups are matched along key demographic variables and other criteria, selection bias remains a threat to internal validity, which limits the generalizability of the results. Nevertheless, the primary advantage of this design is that it allows researchers to eliminate maturation effects, thus distinguishing between effects of the instruction and those of natural developmental maturation and growth.

Sampling

I gathered data from 293 students at Concord High School enrolled in Grade 11 and a random sample of 89 Grade 11 students from a control school, located within a 50-mile radius of the treatment school. I located a control group from another community in New Hampshire with similar instructional quality, school size, and student demographics. Demographic comparison of the two communities shows a pattern of similarities in size, race, gender, and social class variables (see Table A.1). Both Concord and the control community each have a population of approximately 7,000 families, over 95% White. In Concord, there is a higher percentage of households earning under $50,000 because Concord has a greater number of elderly citizens. Students in both

Table A.1. Comparison of Two Communities: Concord and Control Group.

Characteristics	Concord	Control
Community		
Total population	34,141	26,996
Families with school-age children	7,015	7,109
Race: White	95%	96%
Family Structure		
No. of siblings at home	1.7	1.8
No. of people at home	4.0	4.2
Social Class		
Per capita income	$23,262	$24,367
% under $50K	51%	21%
Average home value	$198,000	$242,000
Father's Occupation		
Knowledge-intensive	27%	22%
Science and technology	18%	22%
Hands-on work	24%	24%
Communication-intensive	18%	15%
Home Media and Technology		
Number of televisions	3	3
Percent receiving cable TV	90%	91%
Daily newspaper subscription	68%	68%
Home computer	90%	96%
Number of magazine subscriptions	2.8	2.8

samples had a balanced proportion of male and female students, and both groups were matched in the racial composition of the communities.

A comparison of parental occupations revealed parity between the two communities. We asked students to write down parental occupations as an indirect measure of socioeconomic status and then coded these using categories identified by the U.S. Department of Commerce. For example, 27% of Concord fathers and 22% of control group fathers are identified as book and business knowledge intensive (includes managerial, finance, legal, government); 18% of Concord and 22% of control group fathers are identified with science and technology intensive jobs (includes computers, engineering);

24% of both Concord and control group fathers are identified with hands-on work (includes military, construction, installation, maintenance); and 18% of Concord and 15% of control group with work that is communication intensive (includes community and social services, education, and managerial). Because of the parallel proportions of mothers and fathers involved in hands-on work, service occupations, and knowledge professions, this data enhances our confidence that the samples, while drawn from two different communities, are similar along key dimensions of race, educational background, employment, and social class.

Other data revealed few differences in the media consumption patterns between the control group and treatment group. Media use indicators showed no significant differences between the control and the treatment group in the number of televisions, videocassette recorders, cable television receivers, and newspaper subscriptions. Since a greater proportion of control group students had a computer in the home (96% compared with 90% of the treatment group, $F(1, 726) = 7.51, p < .001$), we used this variable as a covariate in the statistical analyses performed.

Family-size data suggest that the students receiving media literacy instruction may have a slightly higher proportion of smaller, possibly single-family households. While there are fewer siblings in the treatment group (1.8 for the control group and 1.7 for the treatment group), there are small but statistically significant differences in total household size in the treatment group (control group $M = 4.2$, treatment group, $M = 4.0$, $F(1, 726) = 6.82, p < .01$). Compared to the control community, at the time of this study, Concord probably had a higher proportion of single-parent households.

The control school was also selected because of its similarities in terms of the overall instructional program and the quality of the program in English language arts. The principal of Concord High School had previously served as an administrative leader at the control group school. He recommended the school's participation in the research because of perceived similarities in the quality of the faculty, parental backgrounds, funding priorities in the district, and the overall administration of the school. Like the treatment group, the English language arts faculty at the control school favored heterogeneous grouping and had an outstanding reputation in the state for excellence in achievement. The control school's English 11 curriculum emphasized world literature, and like the Concord teachers, the control school faculty valued a process approach to writing, emphasis on critical thinking, rich discussion, and collaborative learning. Expectations for student learning were high in both schools, according to the instructional leaders who were interviewed. During the testing year, faculty at the control site were excited to be involved in pilot testing a new program of portfolio-based assessment. According to the curriculum coordinator for the school, there was significant enthusiasm for this new evaluation approach, which the faculty had long promoted. Differences in teacher enthusiasm can confound results of quasi-experimental designs and while this research did not formally measure teacher enthusiasm in either the treatment group or the control group, interviews with teachers from both sites gave the indication that faculty were equivalent in their engagement with students and level of morale.

Because data were collected from the entire population of Grade 11 students at Concord High School, the treatment sample included all students enrolled in the regular and special education programs. Because courses of study at this school were heterogeneously grouped, the sample included students with learning disabilities, physical disabilities, and hearing-impaired students. Only students who completed the entire battery of identical pretest and posttest measures (administered in September as a pretest and in May as a posttest) were included in the study. Although we were unable to collect data from the entire population at the control school, we were able to use a random sample, which included students with learning disabilities, physical disabilities, and hearing-impaired students. Students in both the control and treatment samples were an average of 17 years old at the start of the testing, with a range of 16 to 18 years.

Research Procedures

Identical test administration procedures were used for both the treatment and control groups through the use of a written protocol. Students entered a study hall in groups of 30 to 50, accompanied by their classroom teachers. Students received code numbers on the first day of testing and all data collected in this study kept students' names confidential. A female experimenter introduced the study, and each test was implemented individually and collected before the next test was administered. Students all received the critical reading test at the beginning of the testing session. To control for order effects, groups received the other critical analysis tasks (listening, critical viewing, advertising) in a rotated order. The administration of these tests took 90 minutes. Students completed attitude questionnaires during the school day in their English classrooms, under supervision from their classroom teacher.

Measures

I measured students' viewing, listening, and reading comprehension and analysis skills by asking them to respond to four messages: (1) a *Time* magazine article; (2) a National Public Radio (NPR) radio commentary from the program, *All Things Considered*; (3) a television news segment from *Channel One*, the daily news show targeted to teens; and (4) a print alcohol ad, reproduced as a black-and-white copy. Students received a media message, and after reading, listening, or viewing, they completed a set of paper-and-pencil measures that included open-ended and checklist-style questions designed to measure comprehension and message analysis skills. I also measured students' knowledge of media production by showing a short TV ad and asking them to list all the steps involved in the media production process. Finally, I asked a series of attitude questions, including measures of political efficacy. The measures and information about their specific use in the research is included in Chapters 6, 7, and 8.

Coding and Data Analysis Procedures

To assist the researchers in coding student tests, all Concord High School English 11 teachers during the 1998–99 school year filled out the complete battery of tests along with their students at the time of the posttest. This data helped me discover some of the areas of consistency between teachers in terms of their own media analysis skills, which aided in decisions about scoring. Two scorers read a sample of 40 student responses plus teacher responses in preparing a coding protocol. For open-ended questions, specific statements were identified and assigned point values reflecting the quality of the response. Based on this sample, I developed a coding protocol describing specific phrases and ideas and the appropriate point value to be assigned for each of the open-ended responses. Then the coders independently read and scored the data, blind to control-treatment condition. A test of interrater reliability using a random sample of tests revealed a Cronbach's alpha ranging from .89 to .93 for items requiring scoring of open-ended responses.

Reliability and Validity

In assessing the reliability of these measures, we built upon the work of Quin and MacMahon (1995), who conducted a study with 1,500 adolescents in Western Australia to examine levels of media analysis skills. Previous research by our team had adapted these measures for use in a study of Grade 9 students who were involved in a media literacy program in a Massachusetts school (Hobbs & Frost, 1999). The use of a variety of open-ended and checklist instruments in response to a print, visual, video, or audio stimuli, enhances the precision of the measures. For example, the measurement of the comprehension and media-analysis variables offers only a moderate level of precision in capturing distinctions between student responses of better and worse quality because of the need for hand scoring. By contrast, the counts of paragraph length, spelling errors, the checklists for identifying purpose and target audience, the measurement of student attitudes, and knowledge of media production offer a higher degree of precision in producing repeatable results consistently.

To enhance the face validity of the media-analysis instruments, I designed them to resemble the five critical questions model used by teachers at Concord High School. The activity of reading, listening to, or viewing a specific media message and then responding to it by answering a set of questions is roughly parallel to the kinds of instructional tasks that are routine in an English language arts classroom. Many scholars and practitioners have described media literacy by pointing out the importance of being able to identify the author's purpose and point of view and to recognize the use of rhetorical or other message construction techniques (Brown, 1991; Silverblatt & Eliceiri, 1997; Thoman & Jolls, 2005), and so these measures reflect some of the key elements of media literacy emerging among a consensus of scholars and practitioners.

Data Analysis

The data were analyzed with the use of analysis of covariance (ANCOVA) using the Minitab statistical program. In this analysis, the pretest scores for each variable served as a covariate and the posttest scores were the dependent measures. The analysis of covariance provides an ability to control for initial differences in the two groups, which is a characteristic typical of quasi-experimental designs. It can also be used with unbalanced designs, when sample sizes are unequal. Because pretest variables are usually highly correlated with posttest variables, the ANCOVA design reduces the variability in the posttest scores (Keselman et al., 1998). On all measures, tests for normality and homogeneity of the within-group regressions were conducted to satisfy the assumptions for the analysis of covariance.

Curriculum Resources
Used in English 11

Books

Anderson, M. T. (2002). *Feed*. Cambridge, MA: Candlewick Press.

Atwood, M. (1986). *The handmaid's tale*. New York: Random House.

Bellamy, R. (2003). *Looking backward 2000–1887*. Peterborough, Ontario: Broadview Press.

Bradbury, R. (1967). *Fahrenheit 451*. New York: Simon and Schuster.

Dick, P. (1968). *Do androids dream of electric sheep?* New York: Ballantine.

Faulkner, W. (1957). *As I lay dying*. New York: Vintage.

Hamill, P. (1998). *News is a verb: Journalism at the end of the twentieth century*. New York: Ballantine.

Hiaasen, C. (1998). *Team rodent: How Disney devours the world*. New York: Ballantine.

Huxley, A. (1946). *Brave new world*. New York: Harper & Row.

Junger, S. (1997). *The perfect storm: A true story of men against the sea*. New York: Norton.

Kesey, K. (1962). *One flew over the cuckoo's nest, a novel*. New York: Viking.

Kilbourne, J. (1999). *Deadly persuasion: Why women and girls must fight the addictive power of advertising*. New York: Free Press.

King, S. (1982). *Cujo*. New York: Signet.

Morrison, T. (1987). *Beloved: A novel*. New York: Knopf.

Orwell, G. (1959). *1984*. New York: New American Library.

Postman, N. (1985). *Amusing ourselves to death: Public discourse in the age of show business*. New York: Viking.

Postman, N. (1993). *Technopoly*. New York: Vintage.

Shakespeare, William (2004). *The tempest*. Washington, D.C.: Folger Shakespeare Library.

Shelley, M. (1994). *Frankenstein, or the modern Prometheus*. London: Penguin.

Stark, S. D. (1997). *Glued to the set: The 60 television shows and events that made us who we are today*. New York: Free Press.

Videos

Advertising and the End of the World (1997)

Dreamworlds (1995)

Scanning Television (1991)

The Classics of Political Advertising (1986)

Tough Guise (1999)

Films

All the President's Men (1976)

Bamboozled (2000)

Blade Runner (1982)

Bowling for Columbine (2002)

Frankenstein (1931)

Gattaca (1997)

Good Night, and Good Luck (2005)

The Handmaid's Tale (1990)

High Fidelity (2000)

JFK (1991)

Mad City (1997)

Mary Shelley's Frankenstein (1994)

One Flew Over the Cuckoo's Nest (1975)

A Perfect Storm (2000)

Pleasantville (1998)

Six Degrees of Separation (1993)

The Truman Show (1998)

Wag the Dog (1997)

Young Frankenstein (1974)

Print Media

Adbusters

Brill's Content

Concord *Monitor*

Newsweek

The New Yorker

New York Times

Time

USA Today

U.S. News and World Report

Radio and Television News Media

Countdown with Keith Olbermann

CNN: *Burden of Proof*

CNN: *Time Newsstand*

Meet the Press

National Public Radio: *All Things Considered*

60 Minutes

20/20

"The War of the Worlds" [Orson Welles' broadcast of H.G. Wells' short story]

WEBSITES

Barker, J., & University of California Berkeley Library. (2005). Evaluating web pages: Techniques to apply and questions to ask. Retrieved February 16, 2006, from http://www.lib.berkeley.edu/TeachingLib/Guides/Internet/Evaluate.html

Geib, R. (2002). Mustapha mond's department of propaganda: Brave new world. Retrieved February 16, 2006, from http://www.foothilltech.org/rgeib/english/bnw/culminating_project/

Journalism.org (2006). State of the News Media 2006. Project for Excellence in Journalism and the Committee of Concerned Journalism. Retrieved July 1, 2006 from http://www.stateofthenewsmedia.com/2006/index.asp

Fairness and Accuracy in Reporting (2006). Retrieved July 1, 2006 from http://www. fair.org/index.php

Free Speech Network (2006). The monopolization of media ownership. Retrieved July 1, 2006 from http://www.freespeech.org/fscm2/genx.php?name=special_ report&queue=the_monopolization_of_media_ownership_

Frontline (2001). The Merchants of Cool. Online video retrieved July 1, 2006 from http://www.pbs.org/wgbh/pages/frontline/shows/cool/view/

Media Matters (2006). Media Matters for America. Retrieved July 1, 2006 from http://mediamatters.org/

Media Research Center (2006). Media Research Center: America's Media Watchdog. Retrieved July 1, 2006 from http://www.mediaresearch.org/

Pride, M. (2006). Mike's Blog. Concord, New Hampshire. Retrieved July 1, 2006 from http://www.conmon.com/MT/

References

Adams, J. (1977). *Media planning* (2nd ed.). London: Business Books.

Alvarado, M., & Boyd-Barrett, O. (1992). *Media education: An introduction*. London: BFI Publishing, in partnership with the Open University.

Alvermann, D. E. (2002). *Adolescents and literacies in a digital world*. New York: P. Lang.

Alvermann, D. E., Moon, J. S., & Hagood, M. C. (1999). *Popular culture in the classroom: Teaching and researching critical media literacy*. Newark, DE: International Reading Association; Chicago, IL: National Reading Conference.

American Library Association, & American Association of School Librarians. (1991). *Information literacy: Learning how to learn*. Chicago: American Library Association.

Anderson, M. T. (2002). *Feed*. Cambridge, MA: Candlewick Press.

Anderson, R. (1995). *Consumer culture and TV programming*. Boulder, CO: Westview Press.

Aufderheide, P., & Firestone, C. (1993). *Media literacy: A report of the National Leadership Conference on media literacy*. Washington, DC: Aspen Institute.

Babbie, E. R. (2004). *The practice of social research* (10th ed.). Belmont, CA: Thomson/Wadsworth.

Barker, J. (2005). *Evaluating web pages: Techniques to apply and questions to ask*. Retrieved February 16, 2006, from http://www.lib.berkeley.edu/TeachingLib/Guides/Internet/Evaluate.html

Barthes, R. (1972). *Mythologies*. New York: Hill & Wang.

Barthes, R., & Keuneman, K. P. (1987). *Criticism and truth*. London: Athlone Press.

Baudrillard, J. (1994). *Simulacra and simulation*. Ann Arbor: University of Michigan Press.

Baudrillard, J. (1999). Consumer society. In J. B. Glickman (Ed.), *Consumer society in American history: A reader* (pp. 33–56). Ithaca, NY: Cornell University Press.

Bazalgette, C. (1991). *Media education*. London: Hodder & Stoughton.

Bazalgette, C. (1992). Key aspects of media education. In M. Alvarado & O. Boyd-Barrett (Eds.), *Media education: An introduction* (pp. 199–219). London: BFI Publishing, in partnership with the Open University.

Bell, P. (2004). On the theoretical breadth of design-based research in education. *Educational Psychologist, 39*(4), 243–253.

Boush, D., Friestad, M., & Rose, G. (1994). Adolescent skepticism toward TV advertising and knowledge of advertiser tactics. *Journal of Consumer Research, 21*, 165–175.

Bradbury, R. (1967). *Fahrenheit 451*. New York: Simon & Schuster.

Branston, G. (1991). Representation. In D. Lusted (Ed.), *The media studies book: A guide for teachers* (pp. 104–122). London: Routledge.

Brown, P. (2005). The shadow curriculum. In G. Schwartz & P. Brown (Eds.), *Media literacy: Transforming curriculum and teaching* (pp. 119–139). Yearbook of the National Society for the Study of Education (Vol. 104, pt. 1). Chicago: National Society for the Study of Education.

Bruce, D. (in press). Multimedia production as composition. In J. Flood, S. Brice-Heath, and D. Lapp (Eds.), *Handbook of literacy research: Communicative, visual and performative arts* (Vol. 2). Mahwah, NJ: Erlbaum.

Brucks, M., Armstrong, G., & Goldberg, M. (1988). Children's use of cognitive defenses against television advertising: A cognitive response approach. *Journal of Consumer Research, 14,* 471–482.

Buckingham, D. (1992). English and media studies: Making the difference. In M. Alvarado & O. Boyd-Barrett (Eds.), *Media education: An introduction* (pp. 124–134). London: BFI Publishing, in partnership with the Open University.

Buckingham, D. (1999). Turning on the news. *Journal of Adolescent & Adult Literacy, 43*(3), 250–254.

Buckingham, D. (2003a). Media education and the end of the critical consumer. *Harvard Education Review, 73*(3), 309–327.

Buckingham, D. (2003b). *Media education: Literacy, learning, and contemporary culture.* Cambridge, UK: Polity Press.

Buckingham, D. (2003c). Pedagogy, parody and political correctness. In D. Buckingham (Ed.), *Teaching popular culture: Beyond radical pedagogy* (pp. 63–87). London: Routledge.

Buckingham, D., Grahame, J., & Sefton-Green, J. (1995). *Making media: Practical production in media education.* London: English and Media Centre.

Buckingham, D., & Sefton-Green, J. (1994). *Cultural studies goes to school: Reading and teaching popular media.* London: Taylor & Francis.

Burbules, N. (1998). Rhetorics of the Web: Hyperreading and critical literacy. In I. Snyder (Ed.), *Page to screen: Taking literacy into the electronic era* (pp. 102–122). New York: Routledge.

Burmester, D. (1974). The language of deceit. In H. Rank (Ed.), *Language and public policy* (pp. 40–51). Urbana, IL: National Council of Teachers of English.

Burn, A., & Leach, J. (2004). ICT and moving image literacy in English. In R. Andrews (Ed.), *The impact of ICT on literacy education* (pp. 153–179). London: Routledge Falmer.

Cervetti, G., Pardales, M., & Damico, J. (2001, April). A tale of differences: Comparing the traditions, perspectives and educational goals of critical reading and critical literacy. *Reading Online.* Retrieved May 12, 2006, from www.readingonline.com

Chandler, D. (2002). *Semiotics: The basics.* London: Routledge.

Christel, M., & Krueger, E. (2001). *Seeing & believing: How to teach media literacy in the English classroom.* Portsmouth, NH: Boynton/Cook.

Christenson, P. (1992). Children's perceptions of TV commercials and products: The effects of PSAs. *Communication Research, 9*(4), 491–524.

Cialdini, R. (1988). *Influence: Science and practice* (2nd ed.). Glenview, Ill.: Scott Foresman.

Cohen, J. J. (1996). *Monster theory: Reading culture.* Minneapolis, MN: University of Minnesota Press.

Collins, J. (1998). Media education in Northern Ireland. In A. Hart (Ed.), *Teaching the media: International perspectives* (pp. 57–78). Mahwah, NJ: Erlbaum.

Cook, G. (2002, April 30). Skin tones and racial stereotyping. *Boston Globe,* C1.

Cook, T. D., & Campbell, D. T. (1979). *Quasi-experimentation: Design and analysis issues for field settings.* Chicago: Rand McNally College Publishing.

Cooper, C. R., & Odell, L. (1977). Holistic evaluation of writing. In C. R. Cooper & L. Odell (Eds.), *Evaluating writing* (pp. 3–31). Urbana IL: National Council of Teachers of English.

Crank, V. (2005). "Doing Disney" fosters media literacy in freshmen. *Academic Exchange Quarterly, 9*(3).

Cushman, K. (1992). Essential schools "universal goals": How can heterogeneous grouping help? *Horace 8*(5). Retrieved July 2, 2005, from http://www.essentialschools.org/cs/resources/view/ces_res/9

Davis, J. (1992). The power of images: Creating the myths of our time. Retrieved January 29, 2006, from http://www.medialit.org/reading_room/article80.html

Eagleton, T. (1983). *Literary theory: An introduction.* Minneapolis: University of Minnesota Press.

Eco, V. (1976). *A theory of semiotics.* Bloomington, IN: Indiana University Press.

Education Development Center. (1970). *Man: A course of study.* Washington, DC: Curriculum Development Associates.

Ellsworth, E. A. (1997). *Teaching positions: Difference, pedagogy, and the power of address.* New York: Teachers College Press.

Erikson, E. (1968). *Identity: Youth and crisis.* New York: Norton.

Faulkner, W. (1957). *As I lay dying.* New York: Vintage Books. (Original published 1930)

Feuer, M., & Towne, L. (2006). Scientifically based research. Retrieved February 9, 2006, from http://www.ed.gov/nclb/methods/whatworks/research/page_pg11.html

Field, J. (1988). Skills and strategies: Toward a new methodology for listening. *ELT Journal, 52*(2), 110–118.

Fitzgerald, M. (1999). Evaluating information: An information literacy challenge. *School Library Media Research, 2.* Retrieved May 12, 2006, from http://www.ala.org/ala/aasl/aaslpubsandjournals/slmrb/slmrcontents/volume21999/vol2fitzgerald.htm

Flinders, D. (2003). Qualitative research in the foreseeable future: No study left behind? *Journal of Curriculum and Supervision, 18*(4), 380–390.

Freire, P., & Macedo, D. P. (1987). *Literacy. Reading the word and the world.* South Hadley, MA: Bergin & Garvey.

Fuller, J. (1996). *News values: Ideas for an information age.* Chicago: University of Chicago Press.

Gallup Youth Poll. (2004, October 26). Teens' leisure habits: TV on top. Retrieved February 9, 2005, from http://medialit.med.sc.edu/teenleisurehabits.htm

Gee, J. P. (1996). *Social linguistics and literacies: Ideology in discourses* (2nd ed.). London: Taylor & Francis.

Gee, J. P. (2004). *Situated language and learning: A critique of traditional schooling*. London: Routledge.

Geib, R. (2002). *Mustapha Mond's department of propaganda: Brave new world.* Retrieved February 16, 2006, from http://www.foothilltech.org/rgeib/english/bnw/culminating_project/

Ginsberg, C. (2006). Why Johnny (still can't) read. *Edutopia, 2*(1), 35–39.

Giroux, H. A. (1999). *The mouse that roared: Disney and the end of innocence*. Lanham, MD: Rowman & Littlefield.

Goldman, R. (1992). *Reading ads socially*. London: Routledge.

Gorski, P. (2004). *Teacher action research*. Retrieved January 17, 2006, from http://www.edchange.org/multicultural/tar.html

Grahame, J. (1991). The production process. In D. Lusted (Ed.), *The media studies book: A guide for teachers* (pp. 146–170). London: Routledge.

Haertel, E., & Herman, J. (2004). A historical perspective on validity arguments for accountability testing. In E. Haertel & J. Herman (Eds.), *Uses and misuses of data for educational accountability and improvement* (pp. 1–34). Yearbook of the National Society of the Study of Education (Vol. 104, pt. 2). Chicago: National Society for the Study of Education.

Hall, S. (1980). Encoding/decoding. In S. Hall (Ed.), *Culture, media and language* (pp. 128–138). London: Hutchinson.

Hamill, P. (1998). *News is a verb: Journalism at the end of the twentieth century*. New York: Ballantine.

Hansen, J. (2003). The language arts interact. In J. Flood, D. Lapp, J. Squire, & J. Jensen (Eds.), *Handbook of research on teaching the English language arts* (2nd ed., pp. 1026–1034). Mahwah, NJ: Erlbaum.

Harms, J., & Kellner, D. (2006). Illuminations: Towards a critical theory of advertising. Retrieved February 1, 2006, from http://www.uta.edu/huma/illuminations/kell6.htm

Hart, A. (1998). *Teaching the media: International perspectives*. Mahwah, NJ: Erlbaum.

Hart, A., & Hicks, A. (2002). *Teaching media in the English curriculum*. Stoke-on-Trent: Trentham Books.

Hayakawa, S. I. (1949). *Language in thought and action: A guide to accurate thinking, reading, and writing*. New York: Harcourt Brace.

Hiaasen, C. (1998). *Team rodent: How Disney devours the world*. New York: Ballantine.

Hobbs, R. (1998). The seven great debates in the media literacy movement. *Journal of Communication, 48*(2), 9–29.

Hobbs, R. (2004). A review of school-based initiatives in media literacy. *American Behavioral Scientist, 48*(1), 48–59.

Hobbs, R., & Frost, R. (1999). Instructional practices in media literacy education and their impact on students' learning. *New Jersey Journal of Communication, 6*(2), 123–148.

Hobbs, R., & Frost, R. (2003). Measuring the acquisition of media-literacy skills. *Reading Research Quarterly, 38*(3), 330–355.

Hobbs, R., Stauffer, J., Frost, R., & Davis, A. (1988). How first time viewers comprehend editing. *Journal of Communication, 38*(4), 50–60.

Huxley, A. (1946). *Brave new world.* New York: Harper & Row.

Hyslop, N., & Tone, B. (1988). Listening: Are we teaching it, and if so, how? *ERIC Digest Number 3* (ED295132). Retrieved January 29, 2006, from, http://www.ericdigests.org/pre-928/listening.htm

Jenkins, H. (1992). *Textual poachers: Television fans and participatory culture.* New York: Routledge.

Jenkins, H. (2006). Training kids with skills for participatory culture. *Project NML.* Retrieved February 17, 2006, from http://projectnml.org/node/308

Junger, S. (1997). *The perfect storm: A true story of men against the sea.* New York: Norton.

Kakutani, M. (1997, June 6). How "Green Acres" et al. changed the nation. *New York Times.*

Kellner, D. (1995). *Media culture: Cultural studies, identity, and politics between the modern and the postmodern.* London: Routledge.

Kennedy, M. (1997). The connection between research and practice. *Educational Researcher, 27*(7), 4–12.

Kesselman, H., Huberty, C., Lix, L., & Olejnok, S. (1998). Statistical practices of educational researchers: An analysis of their ANOVA, MANOVA and ANCOVA analyses. Review of Educational Research, 68, 350–386.

Kesey, K. (1962). *One flew over the cuckoo's nest: a novel.* New York: Viking.

Kilbourne, J. (1999). *Deadly persuasion: Why women and girls must fight the addictive power of advertising.* New York: Free Press.

Kinzer, C. K., & Leander, K. (2003). Technology and the language arts: Implications of an expanded definition of literacy. In J. Flood, D. Lapp, J. Squire & J. Jensen (Eds.), *Handbook of research on teaching the English language arts* (2nd ed., pp. 546–565). Mahwah, NJ: Erlbaum.

Kist, W. (2005). *New literacies in action: Teaching and learning in multiple media.* New York: Teachers College Press.

Kluger, J. (1997, September 8). Mosquitoes get deadly. *Time.*

Koschmann, T., Ostwald, J., & Stahl, G. (1998). *Shouldn't we really be studying practice?* Presentation at International Conference on the Learning Sciences (ICLS), Seattle, WA. Retrieved April 14, 2005, from http://www.cis.drexel.edu/faculty/gerry/publications/conferences/1998/icls98/ICLS%20Workshop.html

Kovach, B., & Rosenstiel, T. (2001). *The elements of journalism: What newspeople should know and the public should expect.* New York: Crown Publishers.

Kress, G. R. (1988). *Communication and culture: An introduction.* Kensington, NSW, Australia: New South Wales University Press.

Larose, S., & Boivin, M. (1998). Attachment to parents, social support expectations, and socioemotional adjustment during the high school-college transition. *Journal of Research on Adolescence, 8*(1), 1–27.

Lewis, J., & Jhally, S. (1998). The struggle over media literacy. *Journal of Communication, 48*(1), 109–120.

Lippmann, W. (1922). *Public opinion.* New York: Harcourt.

Livingstone, S. M. (2003). The changing nature and uses of media literacy. *Media*

Culture Online. Retrieved February 12, 2006, from http://www.mediaculture-online.de/fileadmin/bibliothek/livingstone_changing_nature/livingstone_changing_nature.pdf

Loveless, T. (1999). *The tracking wars: State reform meets school policy.* Washington, DC: Brookings Institution Press.

Lucas, S. R. (1999). *Tracking inequality: Stratification and mobility in American high schools.* New York: Teachers College Press.

Luke, A. (1995). Text and discourse analysis in education: An introduction to critical discourse analysis. *Review of Research in Education, 21,* 1–48.

Luke, C. (1997). Media literacy and cultural studies. In S. Muspratt, A. Luke, & P. Freebody (Eds.), *Constructing critical literacies: Teaching and learning textual practice* (pp. 19–49). Cresskill, NJ: Hampton Press.

Luke, C. (2003). Pedagogy and authority: Lessons from feminist and cultural studies, postmodernism and feminist pedagogy. In D. Buckingham (Ed.), *Teaching popular culture: Beyond radical pedagogy* (pp. 18–41). London: Routledge.

Manoff, R. K., & Schudson, M. (1986). *Reading the news: A Pantheon guide to popular culture.* New York: Pantheon Books.

Masterman, L. (1985). *Teaching the media.* London: Comedia.

McChesney, R. (2004). *The problem of the media: U.S. communication politics in the twenty-first century.* New York: Monthly Review Press.

McDonnell, L. (2005). Assessment and accountability from the policymaker's perspective. In J. Herman & E. Haertel (Eds.), *Uses and misuses of data for educational accountability and improvement* (pp. 35–51). Yearbook of the National Society for the Study of Education (Vol. 104, pt. 2). Chicago: National Society for the Study of Education.

McLaughlin, M., & DeVogel, G. (2004). Critical literacy as comprehension: Expanding reader response. *Journal of Adolescent & Adult Literacy, 48*(1), 52–62.

McLuhan, M. (1964). *Understanding media; the extensions of man.* New York: McGraw-Hill.

Messaris, P. (1994). *Visual literacy: Image, mind and reality.* Boulder, CO: Westview Press.

Michie, G. (1999). *Holler if you hear me: The education of a teacher and his students.* New York: Teachers College Press.

Morgan, R. (2003). Provocations for a media education in small letters. In D. Buckingham (Ed.), *Teaching popular culture: Beyond radical pedagogy* (pp. 107–131). London: Routledge.

Morris, B. (1989). The television generation: Couch potatoes or informed critics? *English Journal, 78*(8), 35–41.

Morrison, T. (1987). *Beloved: A novel.* New York: Knopf.

Morrow, L. (2003). Motivating lifelong voluntary readers. In J. Flood, D. Lapp, J. Squire, & J. Jensen (Eds.), *Handbook of research on teaching the English language arts* (2nd ed., pp. 857–867). Mahwah, NJ: Erlbaum.

Muncey, D., & McQuillan, P. (1996). *Reform and resistance in schools and classrooms.* New Haven, CT: Yale University Press.

Nairn, A., & Berthon, P. (2005). Affecting adolescence: Scrutinizing the link between advertising and segmentation. *Business and Society, 44*(3), 318–345.

Nathanson, A., & Botta, R. A. (2003). Shaping the effects of television on adolescents' body image disturbance: The role of parental mediation. *Communication Research, 30*(3), 304–331.

National Center for Education Statistics. (2002). The nation's report card: Reading 2002. Retrieved July 12, 2002, from http://nces.ed.gov/nationsreportcard/pdf/main2002/2003521.pdf

National Writing Project & Nagin, C. (2003). *Because writing matters: Improving student writing in our schools.* San Francisco: Jossey-Bass.

New Hampshire Department of Education. (2005). Dropouts and completers. Retrieved January 26, 2006, from http://www.ed.state.nh.us/education/data/DropoutsAndGraduates.htm

New Hampshire Department of Education. (2006). Grades 5–12 Reading Grade Level Expectations and Grade Span Expectations. Retrieved July 1, 2006, from http://www.ed.state.nh.us/education/doe/organization/curriculum/NECAP/Grades%205-12%20Reading%20GLEs%20&%20GSEs%20Version%202006.doc

Nichols, B. (1981). *Ideology and the image: Social representation in the cinema and other media.* Bloomington: Indiana University Press.

Nichols, B. (1991). *Representing reality: Issues and concepts in documentary.* Bloomington: Indiana University Press.

Nystrand, M. (1997). *Opening dialogue: Understanding the dynamics of language and learning in the English classroom.* New York: Teachers College Press.

Orwell, G. (1959). *1984.* New York: New American Library.

Packard, V. O. (1957). *The hidden persuaders.* New York: D. McKay.

Pederson, R., Golden, J., & Connolly, E. (2003). Report of the Visiting Committee, Concord High School. New England Association of Schools and Colleges. Commission on Public Secondary Schools, Concord, NH.

Perkins, D. (1993). Teaching for understanding. *American Educator, 17*(3), 8, 28–35.

Peters, C., & Wixson, K. (2003). Unifying the domains of K–12 English language arts curriculum. In J. Flood, D. Lapp, J. Squire, & J. Jensen (Eds.), *Handbook of research on teaching the English language arts* (2nd ed., pp. 573–589). Mahwah, NJ: Erlbaum.

Phelan, J. (1998). Sethe's choice: *Beloved* and the ethics of reading. *Style, 32*(2), 318–333.

Plotnick, E. (1999). Information literacy. Syracuse, NY: ERIC Clearinghouse on Information and Technology. *ERIC Digest* (ED 427777).

Postman, N. (1985). *Amusing ourselves to death: Public discourse in the age of show business.* New York: Viking.

Potter, W. J. (2004). *Theory of media literacy: A cognitive approach.* Thousand Oaks, CA: Sage.

Pressley, M. (1999). Self-regulated comprehension processing and its development through instruction. In L. Gambrell, L. Morrow, S. Neuman, & M. Pressley (Eds.), *Best practices in literacy instruction* (pp. 90–97). New York: Guilford.

Pride, M. (2000). Code of silence: Teen drinking on the rise. *Brill's Content, 3*(2), 49.

Pride, M. (2006, February 2). Question no. 5 (We get letters): How do you decide which letters to print? *Mike's blog.* Retrieved February 17, 2006, from http://www.conmon.com/MT/

Pungente, J. J. (Director), & Marcuse, G. (Producer). (1997). Our constructed worlds: Media environments [Videorecording]. *Scanning television,* no. 3. Toronto: Face to Face Media and Harcourt Brace.

Quart, A. (2003). *Branded: The buying and selling of teenagers*. New York: Basic Books.

Quin, R. (1998). Media education in Western Australia. In A. Hart (Ed.), *Teaching the media: International perspectives* (pp. 107–126). Mahwah, NJ: Erlbaum.

Quin, R., & MacMahon, B. (1995). Evaluating standards in media education. *Canadian Journal of Educational Communication, 22*(1), 15–25.

Rand Reading Study Group. (2004). *Reading for understanding: Toward a R&D program in reading comprehension*. New York: Rand Corporation.

Reinsch, P. (2006). *High fidelity* [Review of the motion picture]. *Pop Matters.* Retrieved February 7, 2006, from http://www.popmatters.com/film/reviews/h/high-fidelity.shtml

Richardson, V. (1994). Conducting research on practice. *Educational Researcher, 23*(5), 5 –10.

Roberts, D., Christenson, P., Gibson, W., Mooser, L., & Goldberg, M. (1980). Developing discriminating consumers. *Journal of Communication, 30*, 229–231.

Rosenwein, R. (2000). Why media mergers matter. *Brill's Content, 2*(10), 93–95.

Ross, R., Campbell, T., Huston-Stein, A., & Wright, J. C. (1981). Nutritional misinformation of children: A developmental and experimental analysis of the effects of televised food commercials. *Journal of Applied Developmental Psychology, 1*, 329–347.

Rossiter, J., & Robertson, T. (1974). Children's TV commercials: Testing the defenses. *Journal of Communication, 24*, 134–144.

Ruenzel, D. (2004). The SAT and the assault on literature. *Phi Delta Kappan, 86*(3), 247–249.

Ruth, L. (2003). Who has the power? Policymaking and politics in English language arts. In J. Flood, D. Lapp, J. Squire, & J. Jensen (Eds.), *Handbook of research on teaching the English language arts* (2nd ed., pp. 87 –113). Mahwah, NJ: Erlbaum.

Sanders, D., & Tumy, K. (2006). Viewing and representing: AP & pre-AP objectives, TEKS, and activities. Lighthouse Initiative, Texas Education Agency. Retrieved July 1, 2006, from http://www.tealighthouse.org/languagearts/wteksviewing.html

Scholes, R. (1985). *Textual power*. New Haven, CT: Yale University Press.

Scholes, R. (1998). *The rise and fall of English: Reconstructing English as a discipline.* New Haven, CT: Yale University Press.

Scholes, R. (2001). *The crafty reader.* New Haven, CT: Yale University Press.

Schrank, J. (1974). *The seed catalog; a guide to teaching/learning materials*. Boston: Beacon Press.

Schudson, M. (1984). *Advertising, the uneasy persuasion: Its dubious impact on American society.* New York: Basic Books.

Schudson, M. (1995). *The power of news*. Cambridge, MA: Harvard University Press.

Schwartz, T. (1973). *The responsive chord.* Garden City, NY: Anchor Press.

Scott, E., & Jones, A. (2002). Al Gore and the "embellishment" issue: Press coverage of the Gore presidential campaign. Cambridge, MA: Kennedy School of Government.

Sebesta, S., & Monson, D. (2003). Reading preferences. In J. Flood, D. Lapp, J. Squire, & J. Jensen (Eds.), *Handbook of research on teaching the English language arts* (2nd ed., pp. 835–847). Mahwah, NJ: Erlbaum.

Semali, L. (2000). *Literacy in multimedia America: Integrating media education across the curriculum*. New York: Falmer Press.

Shalit, R. (1999, September 27). The return of the hidden persuaders. Retrieved May 12, 2006, from *Salon Magazine*, from http://www.salon.com/media/col/shal/1999/09/27/persuaders/index.html

Shelley, M. (1994). *Frankenstein, or the modern Prometheus*. London: Penguin. (Original work published 1818)

Sheng, H. J. (2000). A cognitive model for teaching reading comprehension. *English Teaching Forum, 38 (4)*. Retrieved January 11, 2006, from http://exchanges.state.gov/forum/vols/vol38/no4/p12.htm

Siepmann, C. A. (1950). *Radio, television, and society*. New York: Oxford University Press.

Silverblatt, A. (1995). *Media literacy: Keys to interpreting media messages*. Westport, CT: Praeger.

Silverblatt, A., & Eliceiri, E. M. E. (1997). *Dictionary of media literacy*. Westport, CT: Greenwood Press.

Sizer, T. R. (1984). *Horace's compromise: The dilemma of the American high school*. Boston: Houghton Mifflin.

Sizer, T. R. (1996). *Horace's hope: What works for the American high school*. Boston: Houghton Mifflin.

Slater, M., Rounder, D., Murphy, K., Beavais, F., Van Leuven, J., & Domenech-Rodriguez, M. (1996). Adolescent counter-arguing of TV beer advertisements: Evidence for effectiveness of alcohol education and critical viewing discussions. *Journal of Drug Education, 26*(2), 143–158.

Stark, S. D. (1997). *Glued to the set: The 60 television shows and events that made us who we are today*. New York: Free Press.

Taylor, C. (1998, August 5). Team rodent: How Disney devours the world [Book review]. *Salon Magazine* Retrieved January 2, 2006, from http://www.salon.com/books/sneaks/1998/08/05sneaks.html

Thoman, E., & Jolls, T. (2005). Media literacy education: Lessons from the Center for Media Literacy. In G. Schwartz & P. U. Brown (Eds.), *Media literacy: Transforming curriculum and teaching* (Vol. 104, pp. 180–205). Malden, MA: National Society for the Study of Education.

Thorkildsen, T. (2002). Literacy as a lifestyle: Negotiating the curriculum to facilitate motivation. *Reading and Writing Quarterly, 18*, 321–341.

Tobin, J. J. (2000). *"Good guys don't wear hats": Children's talk about the media*. New York: Teachers College Press.

Torney-Purta, J. (2004). Adolescents' political socialization in changing contexts: An international study in the spirit of Nevitt Sanford. *Political Psychology, 25*(3), 465–478.

Tugend, A. (2003, March). Reading between the lines. *American Journalism Review* Retrieved July 5, 2005, from http://www.ajr.org/article_printable.asp?id=2797

Turnbull, S. (2003). Dealing with feeling: Why girl number twenty still doesn't answer. In D. Buckingham (Ed.), *Teaching popular culture: Beyond radical pedagogy* (pp. 88–106). London: Routledge.

Tyner, K. R. (1998). *Literacy in a digital world: Teaching and learning in the age of information*. Mahwah, NJ: Erlbaum.

U.S. Bureau of the Census. (1995). New Hampshire's population projections, 1994 to 2025. Retrieved January 2, 2005, from http://www.census.gov/population/projections/state/9525rank/nhprsrel.txt

Walberg, H. J., Reynolds, A. J., & Wang, M. C. (Eds.). (2004). *Can unlike students learn together? Grade retention, tracking, and grouping*. Greenwich, CT: Information Age.

Watson, K., Barnes, M. E., Gallo, T., Osborn, B., Learned, M., Scott Newman Center, et al. (1992). *Adsmarts* [Videorecording]. Los Angeles, CA: Scott Newman Center and Center for Media Literacy.

Williams, R. (1975). *Television: Technology and cultural form*. New York: Schocken Books.

Williamson, J. (1981/2). How does girl number twenty understand ideology? *Screen Education, 40*, 80–87.

Witkin, B., & Trochim, W. (1997). Toward a synthesis of listening constructs: A concept map analysis. *International Journal of Listening, 11*, 69 – 87.

Wolbrecht, C., & Campbell, D. E. (2005). *Do women politicians lead adolescent girls to be more politically engaged? A cross-national study of political role models*. Paper presented at the annual meeting of the American Political Science Association, Washington, DC.

Young, B. (1990). *Television advertising and children*. Oxford, UK: Clarendon Press.

Zorfass, J., & Copel, H. (1995). The I-search unit: Guiding students towards relevant research. *Educational Leadership, 53*(1), 48–51.

Index

About the Author

Renee Hobbs is Associate Professor of Communication at Temple University in Philadelphia, where she directs the Media Education Lab. She is a national expert in media education, one of the founders of the organization that hosts the National Media Education Conference. She won a Golden Cable ACE award for *Know TV*, a curriculum sponsored by the Discovery Channel, and has developed media literacy curriculum materials and staff development programs for state agencies including the Maryland State Department of Education and the Texas Education Agency. Her research on the comprehension of television editing techniques won a Top Paper award from the International Communication Association. She has been an advisor on media literacy to the Office of National Drug Control Policy and helped organize two White House conferences on media literacy and substance abuse prevention in 1996 and 2000. She is a coauthor of the language arts textbook series *Elements of Language*.

Hobbs received a B.A. in English Literature and Film/Video Studies and an M.A. in Communication from the University of Michigan, and an Ed.D. from Harvard University in Human Development.